Simple & Delicious

ONE POT

Simple & Delicious

ONE POT

OVER 100 SENSATIONAL RECIPES FOR ONE-POT MEALS

This edition published in 2012
LOVE FOOD is an imprint of Parragon Books Ltd

Parragon
Chartist House
15-17 Trim Street
Bath BA1 1HA, UK
www.parragon.com

ISBN: 978-1-4454-8267-5

Printed in China

Cover Design by Geoff Borin
Photography by Clive Streeter
Home Economy by Angela Drake and Teresa Goldfinch

Notes for the Reader
This book uses both metric and imperial measurements. Follow the same units of measurement throughout; do not mix metric and imperial. All spoon measurements are level: teaspoons are assumed to be 5 ml, and tablespoons are assumed to be 15 ml. Unless otherwise stated, milk is assumed to be full fat, eggs and individual vegetables are medium, and pepper is freshly ground black pepper. Unless otherwise stated, all root vegetables should be washed and peeled prior to using.

Garnishes, decorations and serving suggestions are all optional and not necessarily included in the recipe ingredients or method.

The times given are an approximate guide only. Preparation times differ according to the techniques used by different people and the cooking times may also vary from those given. Optional ingredients, variations or serving suggestions have not been included in the time calculations.

Recipes using raw or very lightly cooked eggs should be avoided by infants, the elderly, pregnant women, convalescents and anyone suffering from an illness. Pregnant and breastfeeding women are advised to avoid eating peanuts and peanut products. Sufferers from nut allergies should be aware that some of the ready-made ingredients used in the recipes in this book may contain nuts. Always check the packaging before use.

Vegetarians should be aware that some of the ready-made ingredients used in the recipes in this book may contain animal products. Always check the packaging before use.

Contents

Introduction

Wonderfully tasty, incredibly easy and packed with nutrients, one-pot cooking is almost too good to be true. What's more, there is an amazing range of different dishes, so you can extend your repertoire of family meals almost effortlessly. Winter warmers, such as stews, casseroles and meal-in-a-bowl soups, are classic one-pot dishes, but there are many other equally trouble-free meals that can be prepared in a single pan, wok or roasting tin from risottos to curries and from pot roasts to gratins. Food cooked in a foil or paper parcel doesn't even require a pot.

Stews and casseroles made with meat and poultry are probably most people's favourite one-pot dishes and these feature in cuisines around the world from North African tagines to Louisiana jambalaya. Many of them use less expensive cuts, making one-pot cooking particularly economical. Fish and seafood also make great one-pot dishes, whether rich mixed stews or quick and easy griddled steaks. The variety of vegetarian options is just as extensive and recipes feature all kinds of vegetables, pulses and mushrooms in casseroles, bakes and rice dishes.

There are many other advantages to one-pot dishes. Cooking everything together simplifies family mealtime. You don't have to remember when to start preparing side dishes so that everything is ready at the right time and there's no risk of overlooking one component of the meal until it's too late. If you're making a slow-cooked stew or casserole, you can safely leave it to simmer gently and do something else or just put your feet up. You use less fuel to heat the food than you would with several different pans which is good for both the family budget and the planet. When the meal has been eaten and what you really want to do is relax, there is less washing up to be done, rather than a stack of pans waiting in the sink.

Equipment

More or less everything you will require for one-pot cooking, whether stewing, poaching, roasting, pot-roasting, braising or stir-frying, will already be in your kitchen. Whatever type of cooking you're doing it's worth buying the best quality pans you can afford and those with a good, thick base are essential for slow-cooked stews and soups and dishes with ingredients such as eggs or rice that stick easily. Lightweight, flimsy pans don't distribute the heat evenly and food is liable to scorch. Do make sure that you use the appropriate size. If the ingredients are crammed into a pan that is too small, they may not all cook fully and you might have to increase the cooking time. They will be difficult to stir and can easily overflow. On the other hand, if you use a pan that is too big, a lot of liquid is likely to evaporate, causing the meal to dry out. Before you start, check whether the dish will be finished in the oven after initial cooking on the hob. If so, a flameproof casserole is more suitable than an ordinary saucepan.

A wide range of cookware that is also suitable for serving is available and is a great timesaver when it comes to clearing up after the meal. Cast-iron casseroles colourfully coated in enamel are attractive and very practical as they can be used on the hob and in the oven. They cook evenly and come in a wide variety of sizes, but large ones are very heavy to lift, even when empty. Casseroles made from ovenproof glass and earthenware are lighter to handle and can be used for both cooking and serving, but are generally not flameproof. They come in many different sizes and shapes and some are designed to co-ordinate with tableware.

Like saucepans, frying pans should have a heavy base to ensure even distribution of heat. Although you can stir-fry in a frying pan, a wok is easier to use. Make sure that you buy the right type; if you cook on an electric hob, you will need a wok with a flat base. It is a matter of personal taste whether you choose pans with a non-stick coating.

They are useful for dishes with ingredients that are inclined to stick but some coatings cannot withstand high temperatures and are therefore less useful for browning meat and for stir-frying.

Traditional metal roasting tins are usually rectangular. Those made of earthenware or ovenproof glass, which take longer to heat up, may be other shapes including oval. As with saucepans, it is important to use the right size. If the tin is too large, ingredients may burn and the interior of the oven is likely to be thoroughly spattered with oil or fat. If it is too small, some ingredients may be undercooked when others are ready. Do check that the tin will fit in your oven before you buy.

Vegetable Stock

Makes: about 2 litres/3½ pints

Ingredients

2 tbsp sunflower oil

115 g/4 oz onion, finely chopped

40 g/1½ oz leek, finely chopped

115 g/4 oz carrots, finely chopped

4 celery sticks, finely chopped

85 g/3 oz fennel, finely chopped

1 small tomato, finely chopped

2.25 litres/4 pints water

1 bouquet garni

Heat the oil in a large saucepan. Add the onion and leek and cook over a low heat, stirring occasionally, for 5 minutes, until softened. Add the remaining vegetables, cover and cook for 10 minutes. Add the water and bouquet garni, bring to the boil and simmer for 20 minutes.

Strain the stock into a bowl, leave to cool, cover and store in the refrigerator. Use immediately or freeze in portions for up to 3 months.

Fish Stock

Makes: about 1.3 litres/2¼ pints

Ingredients

650 g/1 lb 7 oz white fish heads, bones and trimmings, rinsed

1 onion, sliced

2 celery sticks, chopped

1 carrot, sliced

1 bay leaf

4 fresh parsley sprigs

4 black peppercorns

½ lemon, sliced

1.3 litres/2¼ pints water

125 ml/4 fl oz dry white wine

Cut out and discard the gills from any fish heads, then place the heads, bones and trimmings in a saucepan. Add all the remaining ingredients and gradually bring to the boil, skimming off the foam that rises to the surface. Partially cover and simmer for 25 minutes.

Strain the stock without pressing down on the contents of the sieve. Leave to cool, cover and store in the refrigerator. Use immediately or freeze in portions for up to 3 months.

Chicken Stock

Makes: about 2.5 litres/4½ pints

Ingredients

1.3 kg/3 lb chicken wings and necks

2 onions, cut into wedges

4 litres/7 pints water

2 carrots, coarsely chopped

2 celery sticks, coarsely chopped

10 fresh parsley sprigs

4 fresh thyme sprigs

2 bay leaves

10 black peppercorns

Put the chicken wings and necks and the onions in a large saucepan and cook over a low heat, stirring frequently, until lightly browned.

Add the water and stir well to scrape off any sediment from the base of the pan. Gradually bring to the boil, skimming off the foam that rises to the surface. Add all the remaining ingredients, partially cover and simmer for 3 hours.

Strain the stock into a bowl, leave to cool, cover and store in the refrigerator. When cold, remove and discard the layer of fat from the surface. Use immediately or freeze in portions for up to 6 months.

Beef Stock

Makes: about 1.7 litres/3 pints

Ingredients

1 kg/2 lb 4 oz beef marrow bones, sawn into 7.5-cm/3-inch pieces

650 g/1 lb 7 oz stewing steak in a single piece

2.8 litres/5 pints water

4 cloves

2 onions, halved

2 celery sticks, coarsely chopped

8 black peppercorns

1 bouquet garni

Place the bones in the base of a large saucepan and put the meat on top. Add the water and gradually bring to the boil, skimming off the foam that rises to the surface.

Press a clove into each onion half and add to the pan with the celery, peppercorns and bouquet garni. Partially cover and simmer for 3 hours. Remove the meat and simmer for 1 hour more.

Strain the stock into a bowl, leave to cool, cover and store in the refrigerator. When cold, remove and discard the layer of fat from the surface. Use immediately or freeze in portions for up to 6 months.

1

Vegetarian

Chunky Vegetable Soup

serves 6

2 carrots, sliced

1 onion, diced

1 garlic clove, crushed

350 g/12 oz new potatoes, diced

2 celery sticks, sliced

115 g/4 oz closed-cup mushrooms, quartered

400 g/14 oz canned chopped tomatoes in tomato juice

600 ml/1 pint vegetable stock

1 bay leaf

1 tsp dried mixed herbs or 1 tbsp chopped fresh mixed herbs

85 g/3 oz sweetcorn kernels, frozen or canned, drained

55 g/2 oz green cabbage, shredded

pepper

crusty wholemeal or white bread rolls, to serve

Put the carrots, onion, garlic, potatoes, celery, mushrooms, tomatoes and stock into a large saucepan. Stir in the bay leaf and herbs. Bring to the boil, then reduce the heat, cover and simmer for 25 minutes.

Add the sweetcorn and cabbage and return to the boil. Reduce the heat, cover and simmer for 5 minutes, or until the vegetables are tender. Remove and discard the bay leaf. Season to taste with pepper.

Ladle into warmed bowls and serve at once with crusty bread rolls.

Ribollita

serves 4

3 tbsp olive oil

2 medium red onions, roughly chopped

3 carrots, sliced

3 celery sticks, roughly chopped

3 garlic cloves, chopped

1 tbsp chopped fresh thyme

400 g/14 oz canned cannellini beans, drained and rinsed

400 g/14 oz canned chopped tomatoes

600 ml/1 pint water or vegetable stock

2 tbsp chopped fresh parsley

500 g/1 lb 2 oz cavolo nero or Savoy cabbage, trimmed and sliced

1 small day-old ciabatta loaf, torn into small pieces

salt and pepper

extra virgin olive oil, to serve

Heat the oil in a large saucepan and cook the onions, carrots and celery for 10–15 minutes, stirring frequently. Add the garlic, thyme, and salt and pepper to taste. Continue to cook for a further 1–2 minutes, until the vegetables are golden and caramelized.

Add the cannellini beans to the pan and pour in the tomatoes. Add enough of the water to cover the vegetables.

Bring to the boil and simmer for 20 minutes. Add the parsley and cavolo nero and cook for a further 5 minutes.

Stir in the bread and add a little more water, if needed. The consistency should be thick.

Taste and adjust the seasoning, if needed. Ladle into warmed serving bowls and serve hot, drizzled with extra virgin olive oil.

Vegetarian Paella

serves 6

½ tsp saffron threads

2 tbsp hot water

6 tbsp olive oil

1 Spanish onion, sliced

3 garlic cloves, crushed

1 red pepper, deseeded and sliced

1 orange pepper, deseeded and sliced

1 large aubergine, cubed

200 g/7 oz medium-grain paella rice

600 ml/1 pint vegetable stock

450 g/1 lb tomatoes, peeled and chopped

115 g/4 oz button mushrooms, sliced

115 g/4 oz French beans, halved

400 g/14 oz canned pinto beans

salt and pepper

Put the saffron threads and water in a small bowl or cup and leave to infuse for a few minutes.

Meanwhile, heat the oil in a paella pan or wide, shallow frying pan and cook the onion over a medium heat, stirring, for 2–3 minutes, or until softened. Add the garlic, peppers and aubergine and cook, stirring frequently, for 5 minutes.

Add the rice and cook, stirring constantly, for 1 minute, or until glossy and coated. Pour in the stock and add the tomatoes, saffron and its soaking water, and salt and pepper to taste. Bring to the boil, then reduce the heat and leave to simmer, shaking the frying pan frequently and stirring occasionally, for 15 minutes.

Stir in the mushrooms, French beans and pinto beans with their can juices. Cook for a further 10 minutes, then serve immediately.

Ratatouille

serves 4

150 ml/5 fl oz olive oil

2 onions, sliced

2 garlic cloves, finely chopped

2 medium-sized aubergines, roughly chopped

4 courgettes, roughly chopped

2 yellow peppers, deseeded and chopped

2 red peppers, deseeded and chopped

1 bouquet garni

3 large tomatoes, peeled, deseeded and roughly chopped

salt and pepper

Heat the oil in a large saucepan. Add the onions and cook over a low heat, stirring occasionally, for 5 minutes, or until softened. Add the garlic and cook, stirring frequently for a further 2 minutes.

Add the aubergines, courgettes and peppers. Increase the heat to medium and cook, stirring occasionally, until the peppers begin to colour. Add the bouquet garni, reduce the heat, cover and simmer gently for 40 minutes.

Stir in the chopped tomatoes and season to taste with salt and pepper. Re-cover the saucepan and simmer gently for a further 10 minutes. Remove and discard the bouquet garni. Serve warm or cold.

Moroccan Stew

serves 4

2 tbsp olive oil

1 Spanish onion, finely chopped

2–4 garlic cloves, crushed

1 fresh red chilli, deseeded and sliced

1 aubergine, about 225 g/8 oz, cut into small chunks

1 tsp ground cumin

1 tsp ground coriander

pinch of saffron threads

1–2 cinnamon sticks

½–1 butternut squash, about 450 g/1 lb, peeled, deseeded and cut into small chunks

225 g/8 oz sweet potatoes, cut into small chunks

85 g/3 oz ready-to-eat prunes

450–600 ml/16 fl oz–1 pint vegetable stock

4 tomatoes, chopped

400 g/14 oz canned chickpeas, drained and rinsed

1 tbsp chopped fresh coriander, to garnish

Heat the oil in a large, heavy-based saucepan with a tight-fitting lid and cook the onion, garlic, chilli and aubergine, stirring frequently, for 5–8 minutes, or until softened.

Add the cumin, coriander and saffron and cook, stirring constantly, for 2 minutes. Bruise the cinnamon stick.

Add the cinnamon, squash, sweet potatoes, prunes, 450 ml/16 fl oz stock and the tomatoes to the saucepan and bring to the boil. Reduce the heat, cover and simmer, stirring occasionally, for 20 minutes. Add the chickpeas to the saucepan and cook for a further 10 minutes, adding more stock if necessary. Discard the cinnamon and serve garnished with the fresh coriander.

Pepper & Mushroom Hash

serves 4

675 g/1 lb 8 oz potatoes,
cut into cubes

1 tbsp olive oil

2 garlic cloves, crushed

1 green pepper, deseeded
and cut into chunks

1 yellow pepper, deseeded
and cut into chunks

3 tomatoes, diced

75 g/2¾ oz button
mushrooms, halved

1 tbsp Vegetarian
Worcestershire Sauce

2 tbsp chopped fresh basil

salt and pepper

fresh basil leaves,
to garnish

crusty bread, to serve

Cook the potato cubes in a large saucepan of lightly salted boiling water for 7–8 minutes. Drain well and reserve.

Heat the oil in a large, heavy-based frying pan. Add the potato cubes and cook over a medium heat, stirring, for 8–10 minutes, or until browned.

Add the garlic and pepper chunks and cook, stirring frequently, for 2–3 minutes. Add the tomatoes and mushrooms and cook, stirring frequently, for 5–6 minutes.

Stir in the Worcestershire sauce and basil and season to taste with salt and pepper. Transfer to a warmed serving dish, garnish with basil leaves and serve with crusty bread.

Roast Summer Vegetables

serves 4

150 ml/5 fl oz olive oil

1 fennel bulb, cut into wedges

2 red onions, cut into wedges

2 beef tomatoes, cut into wedges

1 aubergine, thickly sliced

2 courgettes, thickly sliced

1 yellow pepper, deseeded and cut into chunks

1 red pepper, deseeded and cut into chunks

1 orange pepper, deseeded and cut into chunks

4 garlic cloves

4 fresh rosemary sprigs

pepper

crusty bread, to serve (optional)

Preheat the oven to 200°C/400°F/Gas Mark 6. Brush a large ovenproof dish with a little of the oil. Arrange the prepared vegetables in the dish and tuck the garlic cloves and rosemary sprigs among them. Drizzle with the remaining oil and season to taste with plenty of pepper.

Roast the vegetables in the preheated oven for 20–25 minutes, turning once, until they are tender and beginning to turn golden brown.

Serve the vegetables immediately, straight from the dish or transferred to a warmed serving platter, accompanied by crusty bread, if you like, to mop up the juices.

Potato & Lemon Casserole

serves 4

100 ml/3½ fl oz olive oil

2 red onions, cut into 8 wedges

3 garlic cloves, crushed

2 tsp ground cumin

2 tsp ground coriander

pinch of cayenne pepper

1 carrot, thickly sliced

2 small turnips, quartered

1 courgette, sliced

500 g/1 lb 2 oz potatoes, thickly sliced

juice and grated rind of 2 large lemons

300 ml/10 fl oz vegetable stock

2 tbsp chopped fresh coriander

salt and pepper

Heat the olive oil in a flameproof casserole. Add the onions and sauté over a medium heat, stirring frequently, for 3 minutes.

Add the garlic and cook for 30 seconds. Stir in the ground cumin, ground coriander and cayenne and cook, stirring constantly, for 1 minute.

Add the carrot, turnips, courgette and potatoes and stir to coat in the oil.

Add the lemon juice and rind and the stock. Season to taste with salt and pepper. Cover and cook over a medium heat, stirring occasionally, for 20–30 minutes until tender.

Remove the lid, sprinkle in the chopped fresh coriander and stir well. Serve immediately.

Lentil & Rice Casserole

serves 4

225 g/8 oz red lentils

55 g/2 oz long-grain rice

1.2 litres/2 pints vegetable stock

1 leek, cut into chunks

3 garlic cloves, crushed

400 g/14 oz canned chopped tomatoes

1 tsp ground cumin

1 tsp chilli powder

1 tsp garam masala

1 red pepper, deseeded and sliced

100 g/3½ oz small broccoli florets

8 baby sweetcorn, halved lengthways

55 g/2 oz French beans, halved

1 tbsp shredded fresh basil

salt and pepper

fresh basil sprigs, to garnish

Place the lentils, rice and stock in a large flameproof casserole and cook over a low heat, stirring occasionally, for 20 minutes.

Add the leek, garlic, tomatoes and their can juice, ground cumin, chilli powder, garam masala, sliced pepper, broccoli, baby sweetcorn and French beans to the pan.

Bring the mixture to the boil, reduce the heat, cover and simmer for a further 10–15 minutes or until the vegetables are tender.

Add the shredded basil and season to taste with salt and pepper.

Garnish with fresh basil sprigs and serve immediately.

Vegetable Stew with Pesto

serves 6

1 tbsp olive oil

1 onion, finely chopped

1 large leek, thinly sliced

1 celery stick, thinly sliced

1 carrot, quartered and thinly sliced

1 garlic clove, finely chopped

1.4 litres/2½ pints water

1 potato, diced

1 parsnip, finely diced

1 small kohlrabi or turnip, diced

150 g/5½ oz French beans, cut into small pieces

150 g/5½ oz fresh or frozen peas

2 small courgettes, quartered lengthways and sliced

400 g/14 oz canned flageolet beans, drained and rinsed

100 g/3½ oz spinach leaves, cut into thin ribbons

1 tbsp of ready-made pesto

salt and pepper

Heat the olive oil in a large saucepan over a medium–low heat. Add the onion and leek and cook for 5 minutes, stirring occasionally, until the onion softens. Add the celery, carrot and garlic and cook, covered, for a further 5 minutes, stirring frequently.

Add the water, potato, parsnip, kohlrabi and French beans. Bring to the boil, reduce the heat to low and simmer, covered, for 5 minutes.

Add the peas, courgettes and flageolet beans, and season generously with salt and pepper. Cover again and simmer for about 25 minutes until all the vegetables are tender.

Add the spinach and simmer for a further 5 minutes. Taste and adjust the seasoning and stir in the pesto. Ladle into warmed bowls and serve with the remaining pesto.

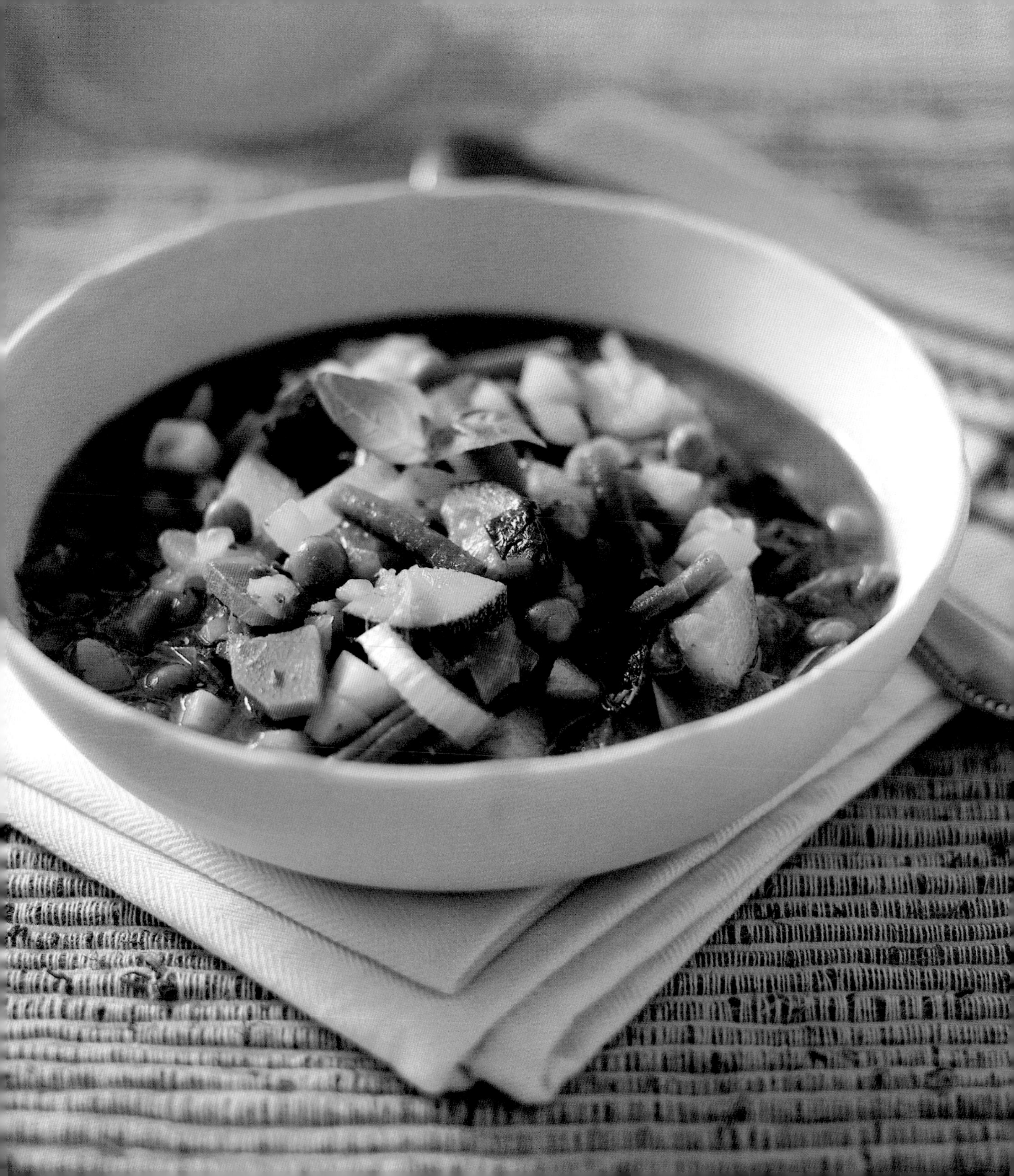

Vegetable Stew with Green Lentils

serves 5

1 tbsp olive oil

1 onion, finely chopped

1 garlic clove, finely chopped

1 carrot, halved and thinly sliced

450 g/1 lb young green cabbage, cored, quartered and thinly sliced

400 g/14 oz canned chopped tomatoes

½ tsp dried thyme

2 bay leaves

1.5 litres/2¾ pints vegetable stock

200 g/7 oz Puy lentils

450 ml/16 fl oz water

salt and pepper

chopped fresh parsley, to garnish

Heat the oil in a large saucepan over a medium heat, add the onion, garlic and carrot and cook for 3–4 minutes, stirring frequently, until the onion starts to soften. Add the cabbage and cook for a further 2 minutes.

Add the tomatoes, thyme and 1 bay leaf, then pour in the stock. Bring to the boil, reduce the heat to low and cook gently, partially covered, for about 45 minutes until the vegetables are tender.

Meanwhile, put the lentils in another saucepan with the remaining bay leaf and the water. Bring just to the boil, reduce the heat and simmer for about 25 minutes until tender. Drain off any remaining water, and set aside.

Allow the stew to cool, then transfer to a food processor or blender and process until smooth, working in batches, if necessary. (If using a food processor, strain off the cooking liquid and reserve. Purée the solids with enough cooking liquid to moisten them, then combine with the remaining liquid.)

Return the stew to the saucepan and add the cooked lentils. Taste and adjust the seasoning, and cook for about 10 minutes to heat through. Ladle into warmed bowls and garnish with chopped parsley.

Parmesan Risotto with Mushrooms

serves 6

2 tbsp olive oil or vegetable oil

225 g/8 oz risotto rice

2 garlic cloves, crushed

1 onion, chopped

2 celery sticks, chopped

1 red or green pepper, deseeded and chopped

225 g/8 oz mushrooms, thinly sliced

1 tbsp chopped fresh oregano or 1 tsp dried oregano

1 litre/1¾ pints vegetable stock

55 g /2 oz sun-dried tomatoes in olive oil, drained and chopped (optional)

55 g/2 oz finely grated Parmesan cheese

salt and pepper

fresh flat-leaf parsley sprigs, to garnish

Heat the oil in a deep saucepan. Add the rice and cook over a low heat, stirring constantly, for 2–3 minutes, until the grains are thoroughly coated in oil and translucent.

Add the garlic, onion, celery and pepper and cook, stirring frequently, for 5 minutes. Add the mushrooms and cook for 3–4 minutes. Stir in the oregano.

Gradually add the hot stock, a ladle at a time. Stir constantly and add more liquid as the rice absorbs each addition. Increase the heat to medium so that the liquid bubbles. Cook for 20 minutes, or until all the liquid is absorbed and the rice is creamy. Add the sun-dried tomatoes, if using, 5 minutes before the end of the cooking time and season to taste with salt and pepper.

Remove the risotto from the heat and stir in half the Parmesan until it melts. Transfer the risotto to warmed bowls. Top with the remaining cheese, garnish with flat-leaf parsley and serve immediately.

Risotto with Artichoke Hearts

serves 4

225 g/8 oz canned artichoke hearts

1 tbsp olive oil

40 g/1½ oz butter

1 small onion, finely chopped

280 g/10 oz risotto rice

1.2 litres/2 pints hot vegetable stock

85 g/3 oz freshly grated Parmesan cheese or Grana Padano cheese

salt and pepper

fresh flat-leaf parsley, to garnish

Drain the artichoke hearts, reserving the liquid, and cut them into quarters.

Heat the oil with 25 g/1 oz of the butter in a deep saucepan over a medium heat until the butter has melted. Stir in the onion and cook gently, stirring occasionally, for 5 minutes, or until soft and starting to turn golden. Do not brown.

Add the rice and mix to coat in oil and butter. Cook, stirring constantly, for 2–3 minutes, or until the grains are translucent.

Gradually add the artichoke liquid and the hot stock, a ladle at a time. Stir constantly and add more liquid as the rice absorbs each addition. Increase the heat to medium so that the liquid bubbles. Cook for 15 minutes, then add the artichoke hearts. Cook for a further 5 minutes, or until all the liquid is absorbed and the rice is creamy. Season to taste with salt and pepper.

Remove the risotto from the heat and add the remaining butter. Mix well, then stir in the cheese until it melts. Season, if necessary. Spoon the risotto into warmed bowls, garnish with parsley and serve immediately.

Cauliflower Bake

serves 4

500 g/1 lb 2 oz cauliflower, broken into florets

600 g/1 lb 5 oz potatoes, cut into small cubes

100 g/3½ oz cherry tomatoes

salt and pepper

cheese sauce

25 g/1 oz butter or margarine

1 leek, sliced

1 garlic clove, crushed

3 tbsp plain flour

300 ml/10 fl oz milk

85 g/3 oz mixed cheese, such as Cheddar, Parmesan and Gruyère cheese, grated

½ tsp paprika

2 tbsp chopped fresh flat-leaf parsley

Preheat the oven to 180°C/350°/Gas Mark 4. Cook the cauliflower florets and potatoes in a saucepan of boiling water for 10 minutes. Drain and reserve until required.

To make the cheese sauce, melt the butter in a large saucepan. Add the leek and garlic and cook over a low heat for 1 minute. Stir in the flour and cook, stirring, for 1 minute. Remove from the heat, then gradually stir in the milk, 55 g/2 oz of the cheese, the paprika and parsley. Return to the heat and bring to the boil, stirring. Season to taste with salt and pepper.

Transfer the cauliflower and potatoes to a deep, ovenproof dish and top with the cherry tomatoes. Pour the cheese sauce over to cover and sprinkle with the remaining grated cheese.

Cook in the preheated oven for 20 minutes, or until the vegetables are cooked through and the cheese is golden brown and bubbling. Garnish with chopped parsley and serve immediately.

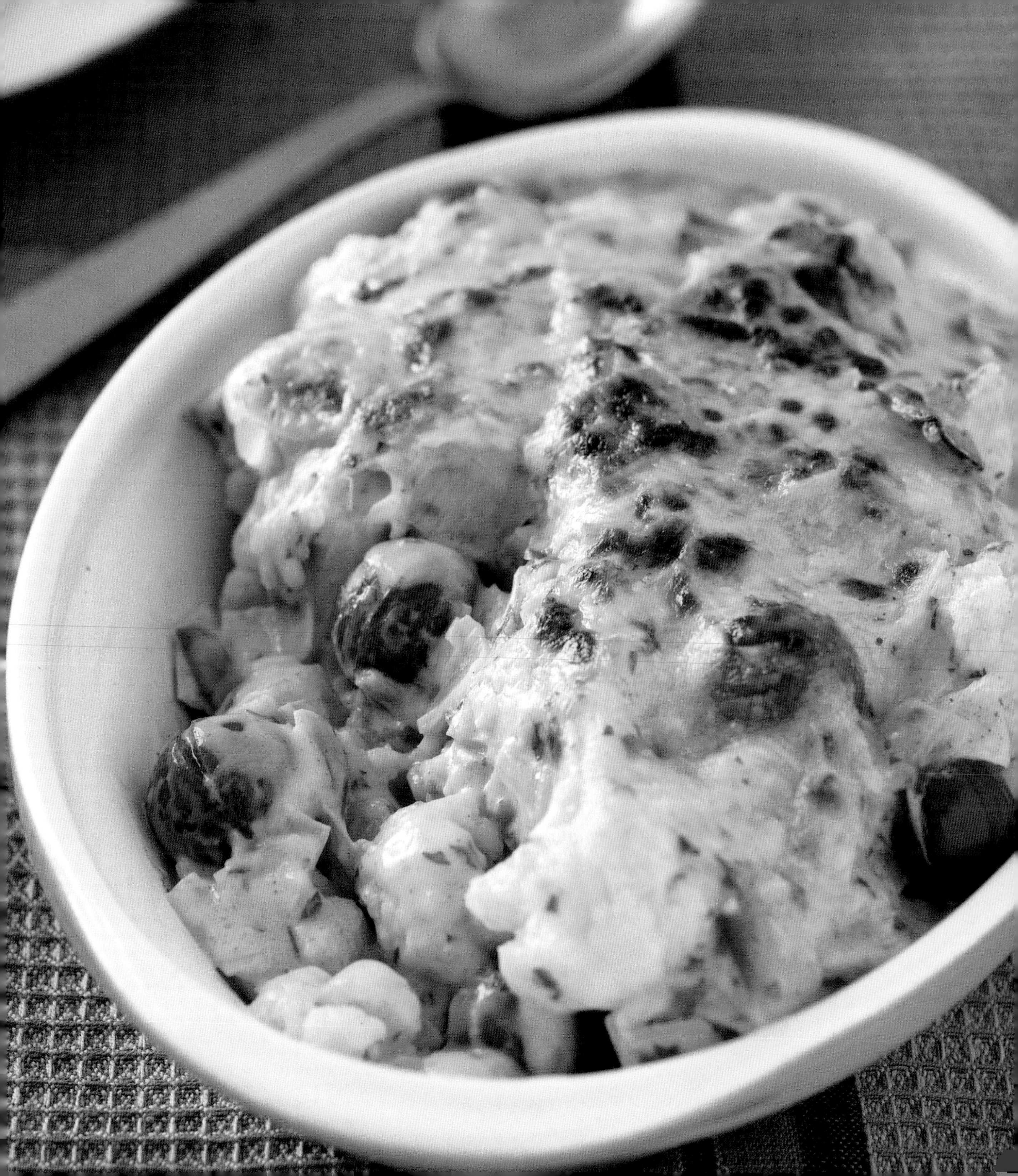

Egg-Fried Rice with Vegetables

serves 4

2 tbsp vegetable or groundnut oil

2 garlic cloves, finely chopped

2 fresh red chillies, deseeded and chopped

115 g/4 oz mushrooms, sliced

50 g/2 oz mangetout, halved

50 g/2 oz baby sweetcorn, halved

3 tbsp Thai soy sauce

1 tbsp palm sugar or soft, light brown sugar

a few Thai basil leaves

350 g/12 oz rice, cooked and cooled

2 eggs, beaten

crispy, fried onions (optional)

Heat the oil in a wok or large frying pan and fry the garlic and chillies for 2–3 minutes.

Add the mushrooms, mangetout and baby sweetcorn and stir-fry for 2–3 minutes before adding the soy sauce, sugar and basil. Stir in the rice.

Push the mixture to one side of the wok. Add the eggs to the wok and stir until lightly set before combining with the rice mixture. Transfer to serving plates and top with the crispy, fried onions, if using.

Aubergine Gratin

serves 2

4 tbsp olive oil

2 onions, finely chopped

2 garlic cloves, very finely chopped

2 aubergines, thickly sliced

3 tbsp chopped fresh flat-leaf parsley

½ tsp dried thyme

400 g/14 oz canned chopped tomatoes

175 g/6 oz mozzarella, coarsely grated

6 tbsp freshly grated Parmesan cheese

salt and pepper

Heat the oil in a flameproof casserole over a medium heat. Add the onion and cook for 5 minutes, or until soft. Add the garlic and cook for a few seconds, or until just beginning to colour. Using a perforated spoon, transfer the onion mixture to a plate.

Cook the aubergine slices in batches in the same flameproof casserole until they are just lightly browned. Transfer to another plate.

Preheat the oven to 200°C/400°F/Gas Mark 6. Arrange a layer of aubergine slices in the base of the casserole dish or a shallow ovenproof dish. Sprinkle with some of the parsley, thyme, salt and pepper. Add layers of onion, tomatoes and mozzarella, sprinkling parsley, thyme, salt and pepper over each layer.

Continue layering, finishing with a layer of aubergine slices. Sprinkle with the Parmesan. Bake, uncovered, in the preheated oven for 20–30 minutes, or until the top is golden and the aubergines are tender. Serve hot.

Potato & Mushroom Bake

serves 4

2 tbsp butter

500 g/1 lb 2 oz waxy potatoes, thinly sliced and parboiled

150 g/5½ oz sliced mixed mushrooms

1 tbsp chopped fresh rosemary, plus extra to garnish

4 tbsp snipped chives, plus extra to garnish

2 garlic cloves, crushed

150 ml/5 fl oz double cream

salt and pepper

Preheat the oven to 190°C/375°F/Gas Mark 5. Grease a shallow, round ovenproof dish with the butter.

Layer a quarter of the potatoes in the base of the dish. Arrange one third of the mushrooms on top of the potatoes and sprinkle with one third of the rosemary, chives and garlic. Continue making the layers in the same order, and finish with a layer of potatoes on top.

Pour the double cream evenly over the top of the potatoes. Season to taste with salt and pepper.

Place the dish in the preheated oven, and cook for about 45 minutes, or until golden brown and piping hot.

Garnish with snipped chives and serve immediately, straight from the dish.

Fish & Shellfish

Fishermen's Stew

serves 6

1.5 kg/3 lb 5 oz live mussels

3 tbsp olive oil

2 onions, chopped

3 garlic cloves, finely chopped

1 red pepper, deseeded and sliced

3 carrots, chopped

800 g/1 lb 12 oz canned chopped tomatoes

125 ml/4 fl oz dry white wine

2 tbsp tomato purée

1 tbsp chopped fresh dill

2 tbsp chopped fresh parsley

1 tbsp chopped fresh thyme

1 tbsp fresh basil leaves, plus extra to garnish

900 g/2 lb white fish fillets, cut into chunks

450 g/1 lb raw prawns

350 ml/12 fl oz fish stock or water

salt and pepper

Clean the mussels by scrubbing or scraping the shells and pulling off any beards. Discard any with broken shells and any that refuse to close when tapped with a knife. Rinse the mussels under cold running water.

Heat the oil in a flameproof casserole. Add the onions, garlic, red pepper and carrots and cook over a low heat, stirring occasionally, for 5 minutes, or until softened.

Add the tomatoes and their juices, the white wine, tomato purée, dill, parsley and thyme, and tear in the basil leaves. Bring to the boil, then reduce the heat and simmer for 20 minutes.

Add the chunks of fish, mussels, prawns and stock and season to taste with salt and pepper. Return the stew to the boil and simmer for 6–8 minutes, or until the prawns have turned pink and the mussel shells have opened. Discard any shells that remain closed.

Serve immediately, garnished with basil leaves.

Fish Stew with Cider

serves 4

2 tsp butter

1 large leek, thinly sliced

2 shallots, finely chopped

125 ml/4 fl oz dry cider

300 ml/10 fl oz fish stock

250 g/9 oz potatoes, diced

1 bay leaf

4 tbsp plain flour

200 ml/7 fl oz milk

200 ml/7 fl oz double cream

55 g/2 oz fresh sorrel leaves

350 g/12 oz skinless monkfish or cod fillet, cut into 2.5-cm/1-inch pieces

salt and pepper

Melt the butter in a large saucepan over a medium–low heat. Add the leek and shallots and cook for about 5 minutes, stirring frequently, until they start to soften. Add the cider and bring to the boil.

Stir in the stock, potatoes and bay leaf with a large pinch of salt (unless the stock is salty) and bring back to the boil. Reduce the heat, cover and cook gently for 10 minutes.

Put the flour in a small bowl and very slowly whisk in a few tablespoons of the milk to make a thick paste. Stir in a little more to make a smooth liquid.

Adjust the heat so the stew bubbles gently. Stir in the flour mixture and cook, stirring frequently, for 5 minutes. Add the remaining milk and half the cream. Continue cooking for about 10 minutes until the potatoes are tender.

Finely chop the sorrel and combine with the remaining cream. Stir the sorrel cream into the stew and add the fish. Continue cooking, stirring occasionally, for about 3 minutes, until the monkfish stiffens. Taste the stew and adjust the seasoning, if needed. Ladle into warmed bowls and serve.

Catalan Fish Stew

serves 4–6

large pinch of saffron threads

4 tbsp almost-boiling water

6 tbsp olive oil

1 large onion, chopped

2 garlic cloves, finely chopped

1½ tbsp chopped fresh thyme leaves

2 bay leaves

2 red peppers, deseeded and roughly chopped

800 g/1 lb 12 oz canned chopped tomatoes

1 tsp smoked paprika

250 ml/9 fl oz fish stock

140 g/5 oz blanched almonds, toasted and finely ground

12–16 live mussels

12–16 live clams

600 g/1 lb 5 oz thick boned hake or cod fillets, skinned and cut into 5-cm/2-inch chunks

12–16 raw prawns, peeled and deveined

salt and pepper

thick crusty bread, to serve

Put the saffron threads in a heatproof jug with the water and leave for at least 10 minutes to infuse.

Heat the oil in a large, heavy-based flameproof casserole over a medium–high heat. Reduce the heat to low and cook the onion, stirring occasionally, for 10 minutes, or until golden but not browned. Stir in the garlic, thyme, bay leaves and red peppers and cook, stirring frequently, for 5 minutes, or until the peppers are softened and the onions have softened further.

Add the tomatoes and paprika and simmer, stirring frequently, for a further 5 minutes.

Stir in the stock, the saffron and its soaking liquid and the almonds and bring to the boil, stirring. Reduce the heat and simmer for 5–10 minutes, until the sauce reduces and thickens. Season to taste with salt and pepper.

Meanwhile, clean the mussels and clams by scrubbing or scraping the shells and pulling out any beards that are attached to the mussels. Discard any with broken shells and any that refuse to close when tapped.

Gently stir the hake into the stew so that it doesn't break up, then add the prawns, mussels and clams. Reduce the heat to very low, cover and simmer for 5 minutes, or until the hake is opaque, the mussels and clams have opened and the prawns have turned pink. Discard any mussels or clams that remain closed. Serve immediately with plenty of thick crusty bread for soaking up the juices.

Sicilian Tuna

serves 4

4 tuna steaks, about
140 g/5 oz each

2 fennel bulbs, thickly
sliced lengthways

2 red onions, sliced

2 tbsp extra virgin olive oil

marinade

125 ml/4 fl oz extra virgin
olive oil

4 garlic cloves, finely
chopped

4 fresh red chillies,
deseeded and finely
chopped

juice and finely grated rind
of 2 lemons

4 tbsp finely chopped fresh
flat-leaf parsley

salt and pepper

Whisk all the marinade ingredients together in a small bowl. Put the tuna steaks in a large, shallow dish and spoon over 4 tablespoons of the marinade, turning until well coated. Cover and leave to marinate in the refrigerator for 30 minutes. Reserve the remaining marinade.

Heat a ridged pan over a high heat. Put the fennel and onions in a separate bowl, add the oil and toss well to coat. Add to the pan and cook for 5 minutes on each side until just beginning to colour. Transfer to 4 warmed serving plates, drizzle with the reserved marinade and keep warm.

Add the tuna steaks to the pan and cook, turning once, for 4–5 minutes until firm to the touch but still moist inside. Transfer the tuna to the serving plates and serve immediately.

Mediterranean Swordfish

serves 4

2 tbsp olive oil

1 onion, finely chopped

1 celery stick, finely chopped

115 g/4 oz green olives, stoned

450 g/1 lb tomatoes, chopped

3 tbsp bottled capers, drained

4 swordfish steaks, about 140 g/5 oz each

salt and pepper

fresh flat-leaf parsley sprigs, to garnish

Heat the oil in a large, heavy-based frying pan. Add the onion and celery and cook over a low heat, stirring occasionally, for 5 minutes, or until softened.

Meanwhile, roughly chop half the olives. Stir the chopped and whole olives into the saucepan with the tomatoes and capers and season to taste with salt and pepper.

Bring to the boil, then reduce the heat, cover and simmer gently, stirring occasionally, for 15 minutes.

Add the swordfish steaks to the frying pan and return to the boil. Cover and simmer for 20 minutes, or until the fish is cooked and the flesh flakes easily, turning once during cooking. Transfer the fish to serving plates and spoon the sauce over them. Garnish with fresh parsley sprigs and serve immediately.

Spanish Fish in Tomato Sauce

serves 4

4 tbsp lemon juice

6 tbsp olive oil

4 swordfish steaks, about 175 g/6 oz each

1 onion, finely chopped

1 garlic clove, finely chopped

1 tbsp plain flour

225 g/8 oz tomatoes, peeled, deseeded and chopped

1 tbsp tomato purée

300 ml/10 fl oz dry white wine

salt and pepper

French beans, to serve

fresh dill sprigs, to garnish

Preheat the oven to 180°C/350°F/Gas Mark 4. Place the lemon juice and 4 tablespoons of the olive oil in a shallow, non-metallic dish, stir well, then season to taste with salt and pepper. Add the swordfish steaks, turning to coat thoroughly, then cover with clingfilm and leave to marinate in the refrigerator for 1 hour.

Heat the remaining oil in a flameproof casserole. Add the onion and cook over a low heat, stirring occasionally, for 10 minutes, or until golden. Add the garlic and cook, stirring frequently, for 2 minutes. Sprinkle in the flour and cook, stirring, for 1 minute, then add the tomatoes, tomato purée and wine. Bring to the boil, stirring.

Add the fish to the casserole, pushing it down into the liquid. Cover and cook in the preheated oven for 20 minutes, or until cooked through and the flesh flakes easily. Serve with French beans and garnished with dill sprigs.

Monkfish Parcels

serves 4

4 tsp olive oil

2 courgettes, sliced

1 large red pepper, peeled, deseeded and cut into strips

2 monkfish fillets, about 125 g/4½ oz each, skin and membrane removed

6 smoked streaky bacon rashers

salt and pepper

slices of olive bread, to serve

Preheat the oven to 190°C/375°F/Gas Mark 5. Cut 4 large pieces of foil, each about 23 cm/9 inches square. Brush them lightly with a little of the oil, then divide the courgettes and pepper among them.

Rinse the fish fillets under cold running water and pat dry with kitchen paper. Cut them in half, then put 1 piece on top of each pile of courgettes and pepper. Cut the bacon rashers in half and lay 3 pieces across each piece of fish. Season to taste with salt and pepper, drizzle over the remaining oil and close up the parcels. Seal tightly, transfer to an ovenproof dish and bake in the preheated oven for 25 minutes.

Remove from the oven, open each foil parcel slightly and serve with slices of olive bread.

Monkfish with Onions & Coriander

serves 4

1 kg/2 lb 4 oz monkfish tail

4 tbsp lime juice

1 garlic clove, finely chopped

1 tsp ground cumin

1 tsp paprika

1 Spanish onion, sliced into rings

2 fresh red chillies, deseeded and finely chopped

1 tbsp chopped fresh coriander

2 tbsp olive oil

salt and pepper

Remove the grey membrane that covers the monkfish tail with a sharp knife, then cut along one side of the central bone to remove the fillet of flesh. Repeat on the other side to remove the other fillet from the bone, then tie the 2 fillets together with string. Transfer the tied fillets to a shallow, non-metallic, ovenproof dish.

Place the lime juice, garlic, cumin and paprika in a bowl, stir to mix, and season to taste with salt and pepper. Spoon the marinade over the monkfish, cover and leave to marinate in the refrigerator for 1 hour.

Preheat the oven to 220°C/425°F/Gas Mark 7. Sprinkle the onion rings, chillies and the chopped coriander over the fish and drizzle with the oil. Roast in the preheated oven for 20 minutes, or until cooked through and the flesh flakes easily. Cut the fish into slices and serve.

Moroccan Fish Tagine

serves 4

2 tbsp olive oil

1 large onion, finely chopped

pinch of saffron threads

½ tsp ground cinnamon

1 tsp ground coriander

½ tsp ground cumin

½ tsp ground turmeric

200 g/7 oz canned chopped tomatoes

300 ml/10 fl oz fish stock

4 small red mullet, cleaned, boned and heads and tails removed

55 g/2 oz stoned green olives

1 tbsp chopped preserved lemon

3 tbsp chopped fresh coriander

salt and pepper

couscous, to serve (optional)

Heat the olive oil in a flameproof casserole. Add the onion and cook gently over a very low heat, stirring occasionally, for 10 minutes, or until softened, but not coloured. Add the saffron, cinnamon, ground coriander, cumin and turmeric and cook for a further 30 seconds, stirring constantly.

Add the tomatoes and fish stock and stir well. Bring to the boil, reduce the heat, cover and simmer for 15 minutes. Uncover and simmer for 20–35 minutes, or until thickened.

Cut each red mullet in half, then add the fish pieces to the casserole, pushing them down into the liquid. Simmer the stew for a further 5–6 minutes, or until the fish is just cooked.

Carefully stir in the olives, preserved lemon and chopped coriander. Season to taste with salt and pepper and serve with couscous, if using.

Seared Scallops in Garlic Broth

serves 4

1 large garlic bulb (about 100 g/3½ oz), separated into unpeeled cloves

1 celery stick, chopped

1 carrot, chopped

1 onion, chopped

10 peppercorns

5–6 parsley stems

1.2 litres/2 pints water

225 g/8 oz large sea scallops or queen scallops

1 tbsp oil

salt and pepper

fresh coriander leaves, to garnish

Combine the garlic cloves, celery, carrot, onion, peppercorns, parsley stems and water in a saucepan with a good pinch of salt. Bring to the boil, reduce the heat and simmer, partially covered, for 30–45 minutes.

Strain the stock into a clean saucepan. Taste and adjust the seasoning, and keep hot.

If using sea scallops, slice in half horizontally to form 2 thinner rounds from each. (If the scallops are very large, slice them into 3 rounds.) Sprinkle with salt and pepper.

Heat the oil in a frying pan over a medium–high heat and cook the scallops on one side for 1–2 minutes, until lightly browned and the flesh becomes opaque.

Divide the scallops between 4 warmed shallow bowls, arranging them browned-side up. Ladle the stock over the scallops, then float a few coriander leaves on top. Serve immediately.

Bouillabaisse

serves 4

100 ml/3½ fl oz olive oil

3 garlic cloves, chopped

2 onions, chopped

2 tomatoes, deseeded and chopped

700 ml/1¼ pints fish stock

400 ml/14 fl oz white wine

1 bay leaf

pinch of saffron threads

2 tbsp chopped fresh basil

2 tbsp chopped fresh parsley

200 g/7 oz live mussels

250 g/9 oz snapper or monkfish fillets

250 g/9 oz haddock fillets, skinned

200 g/7 oz prawns, peeled and deveined

100 g/3½ oz scallops

salt and pepper

Heat the oil in a large pan over a medium heat. Add the garlic and onions and cook, stirring, for 3 minutes. Stir in the tomatoes, stock, wine, bay leaf, saffron and herbs. Bring to the boil, reduce the heat, cover and simmer for 30 minutes.

Meanwhile, soak the mussels in lightly salted water for 10 minutes. Scrub the shells under cold running water and pull off any beards. Discard any mussels with broken shells and any that refuse to close when tapped. Put the rest into a large pan with a little water, bring to the boil and cook over a high heat for 4 minutes. Remove from the heat and discard any that remain closed.

When the tomato mixture is cooked, rinse the fish fillets, pat dry and cut into chunks. Add to the pan and simmer for 5 minutes. Add the mussels, prawns and scallops and season with salt and pepper. Cook for 3 minutes, until the fish is cooked through. Remove from the heat, discard the bay leaf and ladle into serving bowls.

Thai-Style Seafood Soup

serves 4

1.2 litres/2 pints fish stock

1 lemon grass stalk, split lengthways

pared rind of ½ lime, or 1 lime leaf

2.5-cm/1-inch piece fresh ginger, sliced

¼ tsp chilli purée, or to taste

200 g/7 oz large or medium raw prawns, peeled

4–6 spring onions, sliced

250 g/9 oz scallops

2 tbsp fresh coriander leaves

salt

finely sliced red chillies, to garnish

Put the stock in a saucepan with the lemon grass, lime rind, ginger and chilli purée. Bring just to the boil, reduce the heat, cover and simmer for 10–15 minutes.

Cut the prawns almost in half lengthways, keeping the tail intact.

Strain the stock, return to the saucepan and bring to a simmer. Add the spring onions and cook for 2–3 minutes. Taste and season with salt, if needed, and stir in a little more chilli purée if wished.

Add the scallops and prawns and poach for about 1 minute until they turn opaque and the prawns curl.

Stir in the fresh coriander leaves, ladle the soup into warmed bowls, dividing the shellfish evenly, and garnish with chillies.

Moules Marinières

serves 4

2 kg/4 lb 8 oz live mussels

300 ml/10 fl oz dry white wine

6 shallots, finely chopped

1 bouquet garni

pepper

4 bay leaves, to garnish

crusty bread, to serve

Clean the mussels by scrubbing or scraping the shells and pulling off any beards. Discard any with broken shells and any that refuse to close when tapped with a knife. Rinse the mussels under cold running water.

Pour the wine into a large, heavy-based saucepan, add the shallots and bouquet garni and season to taste with pepper. Bring to the boil over a medium heat. Add the mussels, cover tightly and cook, shaking the saucepan occasionally, for 5 minutes. Remove and discard the bouquet garni and any mussels that remain closed.

Divide the mussels between 4 serving bowls with a slotted spoon. Tilt the pan to let any sand settle, then spoon the cooking liquid over the mussels, garnish with a bay leaf, and serve immediately with crusty bread.

Roasted Seafood

serves 4

600 g/1 lb 5 oz new potatoes

3 red onions, cut into wedges

2 courgettes, cut into chunks

8 garlic cloves, peeled but left whole

2 lemons, cut into wedges

4 fresh rosemary sprigs

4 tbsp olive oil

350 g/12 oz unpeeled raw prawns

2 small raw squid, cut into rings

4 tomatoes, quartered

Preheat the oven to 200°C/400°F/Gas Mark 6.

Scrub the potatoes to remove any dirt. Cut any large potatoes in half. Place the potatoes in a large roasting tin together with the onions, courgettes, garlic, lemons and rosemary sprigs.

Pour over the oil and toss to coat all the vegetables. Roast in the oven for 30 minutes, turning occasionally, until the potatoes are tender.

Once the potatoes are tender, add the prawns, squid and tomatoes, tossing to coat them in the oil, and roast for 5 minutes. All the vegetables should be cooked through and slightly charred for full flavour. Transfer the roasted seafood and vegetables to warmed serving plates and serve hot.

Squid Stew

serves 4

750 g/1 lb 10 oz squid

3 tbsp olive oil

1 onion, chopped

3 garlic cloves, finely chopped

1 tsp fresh thyme leaves

400 g/14 oz can chopped tomatoes

150 ml/5 fl oz red wine

300 ml/10 fl oz water

1 tbsp chopped fresh parsley

salt and pepper

crusty bread, to serve

To prepare whole squid, hold the body firmly and grasp the tentacles just inside the body. Pull firmly to remove the innards. Find the transparent quill and remove. Grasp the wings on the outside of the body and pull to remove the outer skin. Trim the tentacles just below the beak and reserve. Wash the body and tentacles under running water. Slice the body into rings. Drain well on kitchen paper.

Heat the oil in a large, flameproof casserole. Add the prepared squid and cook over a medium heat, stirring occasionally, until lightly browned.

Reduce the heat and add the onion, garlic and thyme. Cook, stirring occasionally, for a further 5 minutes until softened.

Stir in the tomatoes, red wine and water. Bring to the boil, then transfer the casserole to a preheated oven, 140°C/275°F/Gas Mark 1 for 2 hours. Stir in the parsley and season to taste with salt and pepper. Serve with crusty bread.

Prawn & Chicken Paella

serves 6–8

16 live mussels

½ tsp saffron threads

2 tbsp hot water

350 g/12 oz cups paella rice

6 tbsp olive oil

6–8 boned chicken thighs

140 g/5 oz Spanish chorizo
sausage, sliced

100 g/3½ oz French beans,
chopped

125 g/4½ oz frozen peas

1.3 litres/2¼ pints fish
stock

16 raw prawns, peeled and
deveined

2 red peppers, halved and
deseeded, then grilled,
peeled and sliced

salt and pepper

35 g/1¼ oz fresh chopped
parsley, to garnish

Soak the mussels in lightly salted water for 10 minutes. Put the saffron threads and water in a small bowl or cup and leave to infuse for a few minutes. Meanwhile, put the rice in a sieve and rinse in cold water until the water runs clear. Set aside.

Heat 3 tablespoons of the oil in a 30-cm/12-inch paella pan or ovenproof casserole. Cook the chicken thighs over a medium–high heat, turning frequently, for 5 minutes, or until golden and crispy. Using a slotted spoon, transfer to a bowl. Add the chorizo to the pan and cook, stirring, for 1 minute, or until beginning to crisp. Add to the chicken.

Add the drained rice, beans and peas and stir until coated in oil. Return the chicken and chorizo and any accumulated juices to the pan. Stir in the stock, saffron and its soaking liquid, and salt and pepper to taste and bring to the boil, stirring constantly. Reduce the heat to low and let simmer, uncovered and without stirring, for 15 minutes, or until the rice is almost tender.

Arrange the mussels, prawns and red peppers on top, then cover and simmer, without stirring, for a further 5 minutes, or until the prawns turn pink and the mussels open. Discard any mussels that remain closed. Taste and adjust the seasoning if necessary. Sprinkle with the parsley and serve immediately.

Laksa

serves 4

1 tbsp sunflower oil

2–3 garlic cloves, cut into thin slivers

1–2 fresh red Thai chillies, deseeded and sliced

2 lemon grass stalks, outer leaves removed, chopped

2.5-cm/1-inch piece fresh root ginger, grated

1.2 litres/2 pints fish or vegetable stock

350 g/12 oz large raw prawns, peeled and deveined

115 g/4 oz shiitake mushrooms, sliced

1 large carrot, grated

55 g/2 oz dried egg noodles (optional)

1–2 tsp Thai fish sauce

1 tbsp chopped fresh coriander

Heat the oil in a large saucepan over a medium heat, add the garlic, chillies, lemon grass and ginger and cook for 5 minutes, stirring frequently. Add the stock and bring to the boil, then reduce the heat and simmer for 5 minutes.

Stir in the prawns, mushrooms and carrot. If using the egg noodles, break into small lengths, add to the saucepan and simmer for a further 5 minutes, or until the prawns have turned pink and the noodles are tender.

Stir in the Thai fish sauce and coriander and heat through for a further minute before serving.

Prawns with Coconut Rice

serves 4

115 g/4 oz dried Chinese mushrooms

1 tbsp vegetable or groundnut oil

6 spring onions, chopped

55 g/2 oz desiccated coconut

1 fresh green chilli, deseeded and chopped

225 g/8 oz jasmine rice

150 ml/¼ pint fish stock

400 ml/14 fl oz coconut milk

350 g/12 oz cooked peeled prawns

6 sprigs fresh Thai basil

Place the mushrooms in a small bowl, cover with hot water and set aside to soak for 30 minutes. Drain, then cut off and discard the stalks and slice the caps.

Heat the oil in a wok and stir-fry the spring onions, coconut and chilli for 2–3 minutes, until lightly browned. Add the mushrooms and stir-fry for 3–4 minutes.

Add the rice and stir-fry for 2–3 minutes, then add the stock and bring to the boil. Lower the heat and add the coconut milk. Simmer for 10–15 minutes, until the rice is tender. Stir in the prawns and basil, heat through and serve.

Meat

Beef Goulash Soup

serves 6

1 tbsp olive oil

500 g/1 lb 2 oz fresh lean beef mince

2 onions, finely chopped

2 garlic cloves, finely chopped

2 tbsp plain flour

225 ml/8 fl oz water

400 g/14 oz canned chopped tomatoes

1 carrot, finely chopped

225 g/8 oz red pepper, roasted, peeled, deseeded and chopped

1 tsp Hungarian paprika

¼ tsp caraway seeds

pinch of dried oregano

1 litre/1¾ pints beef stock

55 g/2 oz tagliatelle, broken into small pieces

salt and pepper

soured cream and sprigs of fresh coriander, to garnish

Heat the oil in a large wide saucepan over a medium–high heat. Add the beef and sprinkle with salt and pepper. Fry until lightly browned.

Reduce the heat and add the onions and garlic. Cook for about 3 minutes, stirring frequently, until the onions are softened. Stir in the flour and continue cooking for 1 minute.

Add the water and stir to combine well, scraping the bottom of the pan to mix in the flour. Stir in the tomatoes, carrot, pepper, paprika, caraway seeds, oregano and stock.

Bring just to the boil. Reduce the heat, cover and simmer gently for about 40 minutes, stirring occasionally, until all the vegetables are tender.

Add the tagliatelle to the soup and simmer for a further 20 minutes, or until the tagliatelle is cooked.

Taste the soup and adjust the seasoning, if necessary. Ladle into warmed bowls and top each with a tablespoonful of soured cream. Garnish with coriander and serve.

Chilli Con Carne

serves 4

750 g/1 lb 10 oz lean stewing steak

2 tbsp vegetable oil

1 large onion, sliced

2–4 garlic cloves, crushed

1 tbsp plain flour

425 ml/15 fl oz tomato juice

400 g/14 oz canned tomatoes

1–2 tbsp sweet chilli sauce

1 tsp ground cumin

425 g/15 oz canned red kidney beans, drained and rinsed

½ teaspoon dried oregano

1–2 tbsp chopped fresh parsley

salt and pepper

sprigs of fresh herbs, to garnish

freshly cooked rice and tortillas, to serve

Preheat the oven to 160°C/325°F/Gas Mark 3. Using a sharp knife, cut the beef into 2-cm/¾-inch cubes. Heat the vegetable oil in a large flameproof casserole dish and fry the beef over a medium heat until well sealed on all sides. Remove the beef from the casserole with a slotted spoon and reserve until required.

Add the onion and garlic to the casserole and fry until lightly browned; then stir in the flour and cook for 1–2 minutes.

Stir in the tomato juice and tomatoes and bring to the boil. Return the beef to the casserole and add the chilli sauce, cumin and salt and pepper to taste. Cover and cook in the preheated oven for 1½ hours, or until the beef is almost tender.

Stir in the kidney beans, oregano and parsley, and adjust the seasoning to taste, if necessary. Cover the casserole and return to the oven for 45 minutes. Serve on a bed of freshly cooked rice, garnished with sprigs of fresh herbs and accompanied by tortillas.

Daube of Beef

serves 6

350 ml/12 fl oz dry white wine

2 tbsp brandy

1 tbsp white wine vinegar

4 shallots, sliced

4 carrots, sliced

1 garlic clove, finely chopped

6 black peppercorns

4 fresh thyme sprigs

1 fresh rosemary sprig

2 fresh parsley sprigs, plus extra to garnish

1 bay leaf

750 g/1 lb 10 oz beef topside, cut into 2.5-cm/1-inch cubes

2 tbsp olive oil

800 g/1 lb 12 oz canned chopped tomatoes

225 g/8 oz mushrooms, sliced

strip of finely pared orange rind

55 g/2 oz Bayonne ham, cut into strips

12 black olives

salt

Combine the wine, brandy, vinegar, shallots, carrots, garlic, peppercorns, thyme, rosemary, parsley and bay leaf, and season to taste with salt. Add the beef, stirring to coat, then cover with clingfilm and leave in the refrigerator to marinate for 8 hours, or overnight.

Preheat the oven to 150°C/300°F/Gas Mark 2. Drain the beef, reserving the marinade, and pat dry on kitchen paper. Heat half the oil in a large, flameproof casserole. Add the beef in batches and cook over a medium heat, stirring, for 3–4 minutes, or until browned. Transfer the beef to a plate with a slotted spoon. Brown the remaining beef, adding more oil, if necessary.

Return all of the beef to the casserole and add the tomatoes and their juices, mushrooms and orange rind. Strain the reserved marinade into the casserole. Bring to the boil, cover and cook in the oven for 2½ hours.

Remove the casserole from the oven, add the ham and olives and return it to the oven to cook for a further 30 minutes, or until the beef is very tender. Discard the orange rind and serve straight from the casserole, garnished with parsley.

Beef in Beer with Herb Dumplings

serves 6

2 tbsp sunflower oil

2 large onions, thinly sliced

8 carrots, sliced

4 tbsp plain flour

1.25 kg/2 lb 12 oz stewing steak, cut into cubes

425 ml/15 fl oz stout

2 tsp muscovado sugar

2 bay leaves

1 tbsp chopped fresh thyme

salt and pepper

herb dumplings

115 g/4 oz self-raising flour

pinch of salt

55 g/2 oz shredded suet

2 tbsp chopped fresh parsley, plus extra to garnish

about 4 tbsp water

Preheat the oven to 160°C/325°F/Gas Mark 3. Heat the oil in a flameproof casserole. Add the onions and carrots and cook over a low heat, stirring occasionally, for 5 minutes, or until the onions are softened. Meanwhile, place the flour in a polythene bag and season with salt and pepper. Add the stewing steak to the bag, tie the top and shake well to coat. Do this in batches, if necessary.

Remove the vegetables from the casserole with a slotted spoon and reserve. Add the stewing steak to the casserole, in batches, and cook, stirring frequently, until browned all over. Return all the meat and the onions and carrots to the casserole and sprinkle in any remaining seasoned flour. Pour in the stout and add the sugar, bay leaves and thyme. Bring to the boil, cover and transfer to the preheated oven to bake for 1¾ hours.

To make the herb dumplings, sift the flour and salt into a bowl. Stir in the suet and parsley and add enough of the water to make a soft dough. Shape into small balls between the palms of your hands. Add to the casserole and return to the oven for 30 minutes. Remove and discard the bay leaves. Serve immediately, sprinkled with chopped parsley.

Beef Stroganoff

serves 4

15 g/½ oz dried ceps

350 g/12 oz beef fillet

2 tbsp olive oil

115 g/4 oz shallots, sliced

175 g/6 oz chestnut mushrooms

½ tsp Dijon mustard

5 tbsp double cream

salt and pepper

freshly cooked pasta, to serve

fresh chives, to garnish

Place the dried ceps in a bowl and cover with hot water. Leave to soak for 20 minutes. Meanwhile, cut the beef against the grain into 5-mm/¼-inch-thick slices, then into 1-cm/½-inch-long strips, and reserve.

Drain the ceps, reserving the soaking liquid, and chop. Strain the soaking liquid through a fine-mesh sieve or coffee filter and reserve.

Heat half the oil in a large frying pan. Add the shallots and cook over a low heat, stirring occasionally, for 5 minutes, or until softened. Add the soaked ceps, reserved soaking water and whole chestnut mushrooms and cook, stirring frequently, for 10 minutes, or until almost all of the liquid has evaporated, then transfer the mixture to a plate.

Heat the remaining oil in the frying pan, add the beef and cook, stirring frequently, for 4 minutes, or until browned all over. You may need to do this in batches. Return the mushroom mixture to the frying pan and season to taste with salt and pepper. Place the mustard and cream in a small bowl and stir to mix, then fold into the meat and mushroom mixture. Heat through gently, then serve with freshly cooked pasta, garnished with chives.

Pork & Vegetable Broth

serves 4

1 tbsp chilli oil

1 garlic clove, chopped

3 spring onions, sliced

1 red pepper, deseeded and finely sliced

2 tbsp cornflour

1 litre/1¾ pints vegetable stock

1 tbsp soy sauce

2 tbsp rice wine or dry sherry

150 g/5½ oz pork fillet, sliced

1 tbsp finely chopped lemon grass

1 small red chilli, deseeded and finely chopped

1 tbsp grated fresh ginger

115 g/4 oz fine egg noodles

200 g/7 oz canned water chestnuts, drained and sliced

salt and pepper

Heat the oil in a large saucepan. Add the garlic and spring onions and cook over a medium heat, stirring, for 3 minutes, until slightly softened. Add the red pepper and cook for a further 5 minutes, stirring.

In a bowl, mix the cornflour with enough of the stock to make a smooth paste, then stir it into the pan. Cook, stirring, for 2 minutes. Stir in the remaining stock and the soy sauce and rice wine, then add the pork, lemon grass, chilli and ginger. Season with salt and pepper. Bring to the boil, then lower the heat and simmer for 25 minutes. Add the noodles to the pan and cook for 3 minutes, add the water chestnuts and cook for a further 2 minutes.

Ladle into serving bowls and serve.

Pot Roast with Potatoes & Dill

serves 6

2½ tbsp plain flour

1 tsp salt

¼ tsp pepper

1 rolled brisket joint, weighing 1.6 kg/3 lb 8 oz

2 tbsp vegetable oil

2 tbsp butter

1 onion, finely chopped

2 celery sticks, diced

2 carrots, peeled and diced

1 tsp dill seed

1 tsp dried thyme or oregano

350 ml/12 fl oz red wine

150–225 ml/5–8 fl oz beef stock

4–5 potatoes, cut into large chunks and boiled until just tender

2 tbsp chopped fresh dill, to serve

Preheat the oven to 140°C/275°F/Gas Mark 1. Mix 2 tablespoons of the flour with the salt and pepper in a shallow dish. Dip the meat to coat. Heat the oil in a flameproof casserole and brown the meat all over. Transfer to a plate. Add half the butter to the casserole and cook the onion, celery, carrots, dill seed and thyme for 5 minutes. Return the meat and juices to the casserole.

Pour in the wine and enough stock to reach one third of the way up the meat. Bring to the boil, cover and cook in the oven for 3 hours, turning the meat every 30 minutes. After it has been cooking for 2 hours, add the potatoes and more stock if necessary.

When ready, transfer the meat and vegetables to a warmed serving dish. Strain the cooking liquid to remove any solids, then return the liquid to the casserole.

Mix the remaining butter and flour to a paste. Bring the cooking liquid to the boil. Whisk in small pieces of the flour and butter paste, whisking constantly until the sauce is smooth. Pour the sauce over the meat and vegetables. Sprinkle with the fresh dill to serve.

Pork & Sausage Bake

serves 4

2 tbsp sunflower oil

25 g/1 oz butter

450 g/1 lb pork fillet or loin,
cut into thin strips

1 large onion, chopped

1 red pepper, deseeded and
sliced

1 orange pepper, deseeded
and sliced

115 g/4 oz mushrooms,
sliced

140 g/5 oz long-grain rice

425 ml/15 fl oz beef stock

225 g/8 oz smoked sausage,
sliced

1/4 tsp ground mixed spice

salt and pepper

2 tbsp chopped fresh
parsley, to garnish

Preheat the oven to 180°C/350°F/Gas Mark 4. Heat the oil and butter in a large, flameproof casserole. Add the pork and cook over a medium heat, stirring, for 5 minutes, until browned. Transfer to a plate.

Add the onion and cook over a low heat, stirring occasionally, for 5 minutes, or until softened. Add the peppers and cook, stirring frequently, for a further 4–5 minutes. Add the mushrooms and cook for 1 minute, then stir in the rice. Cook for 1 minute, or until the grains are well coated, then add the stock and bring to the boil.

Return the pork to the casserole, add the sausage and mixed spice and season to taste with salt and pepper. Mix thoroughly, cover and cook in the preheated oven for 1 hour, or until all the liquid has been absorbed and the meat is tender. Serve immediately, garnished with chopped parsley.

Pot-roast Pork

serves 4

1 tbsp sunflower oil

55 g/2 oz butter

1 kg/2 lb 4 oz boned and rolled pork loin joint

4 shallots, chopped

6 juniper berries

2 fresh thyme sprigs, plus extra to garnish

150 ml/5 fl oz dry cider

150 ml/5 fl oz chicken stock or water

8 celery sticks, chopped

2 tbsp plain flour

150 ml/5 fl oz double cream

salt and pepper

freshly cooked peas, to serve

Heat the oil with half the butter in a heavy-based saucepan or flameproof casserole. Add the pork and cook over a medium heat, turning frequently, for 5–10 minutes, or until browned. Transfer to a plate.

Add the shallots to the saucepan and cook, stirring frequently, for 5 minutes, or until softened. Add the juniper berries and thyme sprigs and return the pork to the saucepan, with any juices that have collected on the plate. Pour in the cider and stock, season to taste with salt and pepper, then cover and simmer for 30 minutes. Turn the pork over and add the celery. Re-cover the pan and cook for a further 40 minutes.

Meanwhile, make a beurre manié by mashing the remaining butter with the flour in a small bowl. Transfer the pork to a platter with a slotted spoon and keep warm. Remove and discard the juniper berries and thyme. Whisk the beurre manié, a little at a time, into the simmering cooking liquid. Cook, stirring constantly, for 2 minutes, then stir in the cream and bring to the boil.

Slice the pork and spoon a little of the sauce over it. Garnish with thyme sprigs and serve immediately with freshly cooked peas and the remaining sauce.

Pork Hot Pot

serves 6

85 g/3 oz plain flour

1.3 kg/3 lb pork fillet, cut into 5-mm/¼-inch slices

4 tbsp sunflower oil

2 onions, thinly sliced

2 garlic cloves

400 g/14 oz canned chopped tomatoes

350 ml/12 fl oz dry white wine

1 tbsp torn fresh basil leaves

2 tbsp chopped fresh parsley

salt and pepper

fresh oregano, to garnish

fresh crusty bread, to serve

Spread the flour on a plate and season with salt and pepper. Coat the pork slices in the flour, shaking off any excess. Heat the sunflower oil in a flameproof casserole. Add the pork slices and cook over a medium heat, turning occasionally, for 4–5 minutes, or until browned all over. Transfer the pork to a plate with a slotted spoon.

Add the onion slices to the casserole and cook over a low heat, stirring occasionally, for 10 minutes, or until golden brown. Finely chop the garlic, add it to the pan and cook for a further 2 minutes, then add the tomatoes, wine and basil leaves and season to taste with salt and pepper. Cook, stirring frequently, for 3 minutes.

Return the pork to the casserole, cover and simmer gently for 1 hour, or until the meat is tender. Snip in the parsley, garnish with oregano and serve with fresh crusty bread.

Red Curry Pork with Peppers

serves 4

2 tbsp vegetable or groundnut oil

1 onion, roughly chopped

2 garlic cloves, chopped

450 g/1 lb pork fillet, thickly sliced

1 red pepper, deseeded and cut into squares

175 g/6 oz mushrooms, quartered

2 tbsp Thai red curry paste

115 g/4 oz creamed coconut, chopped

300 ml/½ pint pork or vegetable stock

2 tbsp Thai soy sauce

4 tomatoes, peeled, deseeded and chopped

handful of fresh coriander, chopped

Heat the oil in a wok or large frying pan and fry the onion and garlic for 1–2 minutes, until they are softened but not browned.

Add the pork slices and stir-fry for 2–3 minutes until browned all over. Add the pepper, mushrooms and curry paste.

Dissolve the coconut in the stock and add to the wok with the soy sauce. Bring to the boil and simmer for 4–5 minutes until the liquid has reduced and thickened.

Add the tomatoes and coriander and cook for 1–2 minutes before serving.

Sausage & Bean Casserole

serves 4

8 Italian sausages

3 tbsp olive oil

1 large onion, chopped

2 garlic cloves, chopped

1 green bell pepper, deseeded and sliced

225g/8 oz canned chopped tomatoes, skinned and chopped or 400 g/14 oz can tomatoes, chopped

2 tbsp sun-dried tomato purée

400 g/14 oz canned cannellini beans

Prick the sausages all over with a fork. Heat 2 tablespoons of the oil in a large, heavy-based frying pan. Add the sausages and cook over a low heat, turning frequently, for 10–15 minutes, until evenly browned and cooked through. Remove them from the frying pan and keep warm. Drain off the oil and wipe out the pan with kitchen paper.

Heat the remaining oil in the frying pan. Add the onion, garlic and pepper to the frying pan and cook for 5 minutes, stirring occasionally, or until softened.

Add the tomatoes to the frying pan and leave the mixture to simmer for about 5 minutes, stirring occasionally, or until slightly reduced and thickened.

Stir the sun-dried tomato purée, cannellini beans and Italian sausages into the mixture in the frying pan. Cook for 4–5 minutes or until the mixture is piping hot. Add 4–5 tablespoons of water if the mixture becomes too dry during cooking.

Transfer to serving plates and serve.

Hearty Winter Broth

serves 4

1 tbsp vegetable oil

500 g/1 lb 2 oz lean neck of lamb

1 large onion, sliced

2 carrots, sliced

2 leeks, sliced

1 litre/1¾ pints vegetable stock

1 bay leaf

sprigs of fresh parsley

55 g/2 oz pearl barley

salt and pepper

Heat the vegetable oil in a large, heavy-based saucepan and add the pieces of lamb, turning them to seal and brown on both sides. Lift the lamb out of the pan and set aside until required.

Add the onion, carrots and leeks to the saucepan and cook gently for about 3 minutes.

Return the lamb to the saucepan and add the vegetable stock, bay leaf, parsley and pearl barley to the saucepan. Bring the mixture in the pan to the boil, then reduce the heat. Cover and simmer for 1½ –2 hours.

Discard the bay leaf. Lift the pieces of lamb from the broth and allow them to cool slightly. Remove the bones and any fat and chop the meat. Return the lamb to the broth and reheat gently. Season to taste with salt and pepper.

It is advisable to prepare this soup a day ahead, then leave it to cool, cover and refrigerate overnight. When ready to serve, remove and discard the layer of fat from the surface and reheat the soup gently. Ladle into warmed bowls and serve immediately.

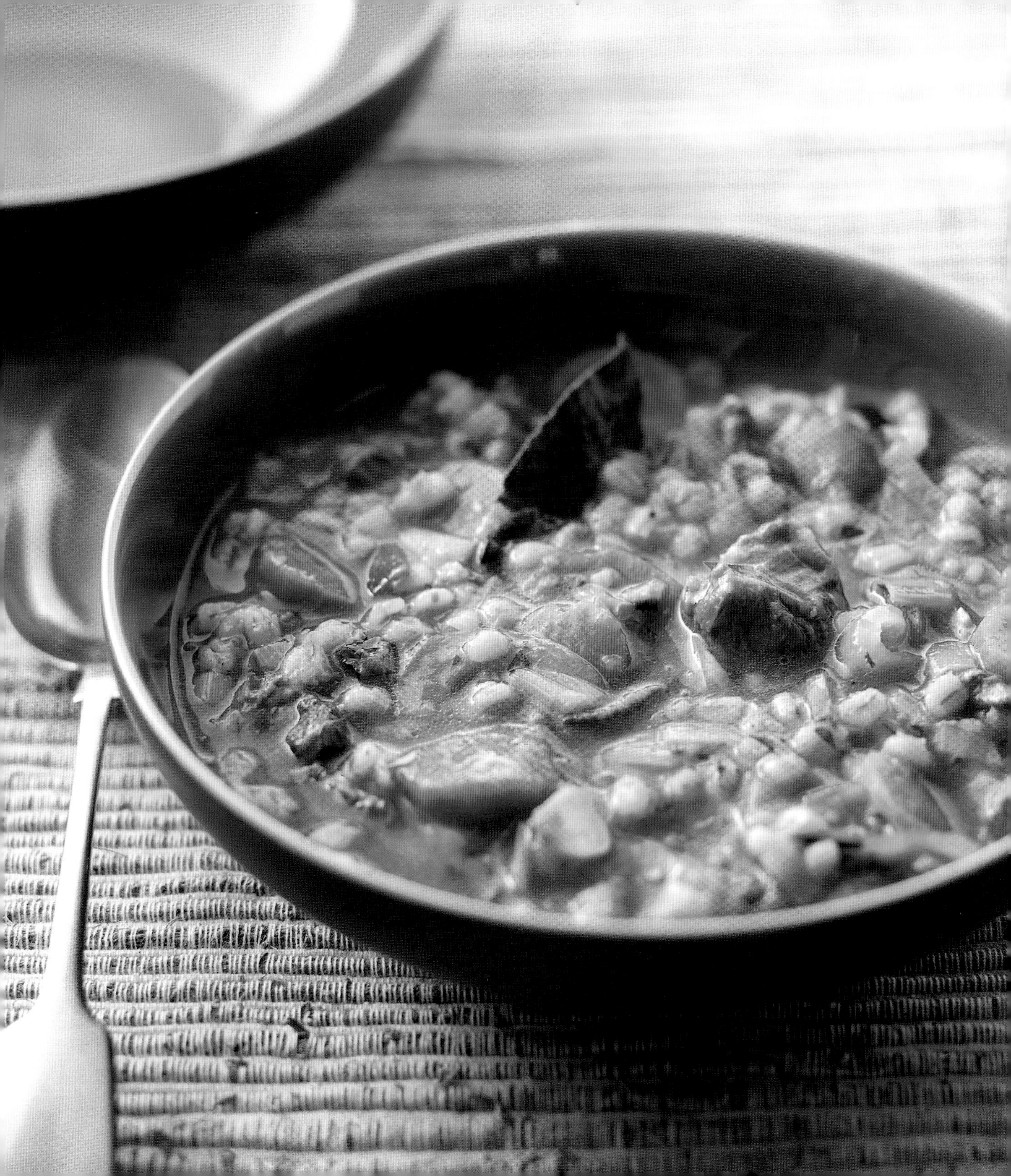

Lamb & Potato Moussaka

serves 4

1 large aubergine, sliced

1 tbsp olive oil

1 onion, chopped finely

1 garlic clove, crushed

350 g/12 oz fresh lean lamb mince

250 g/9 oz mushrooms, sliced

425 g/15 oz canned chopped tomatoes with herbs

150 ml/5 fl oz lamb stock

2 tbsp cornflour

2 tbsp water

500 g/1 lb 2 oz potatoes, parboiled for 10 minutes and sliced

2 eggs

125 g/4½ oz low-fat soft cheese

150 ml/5 fl oz low-fat natural yogurt

55 g/2 oz low-fat mature Cheddar cheese, grated

salt and pepper

Preheat the oven to 190°C/375°F/Gas Mark 5. Lay the aubergine slices on a clean board and sprinkle with salt. Leave for 10 minutes, then turn the slices over and repeat. Place in a colander, rinse and drain.

While the aubergines are standing, heat the oil in a large saucepan. Add the onion and garlic and cook for 3–4 minutes. Add the lamb and mushrooms and cook over a medium heat for 5 minutes, or until browned. Stir in the tomatoes and stock, bring to the boil and simmer for 10 minutes. Mix the cornflour and water together to make a smooth paste, then stir into the saucepan. Cook, stirring constantly, until thickened.

Spoon half the mixture into an ovenproof dish. Cover with the aubergine slices, then the remaining lamb mixture. Arrange the sliced potatoes on top.

Beat the eggs, soft cheese and yogurt together. Season to taste with salt and pepper, then pour over the potatoes to cover. Sprinkle over the cheese and bake in the preheated oven for 45 minutes, or until the topping is set and golden brown. Serve.

Lamb Stew with Chickpeas

serves 4–6

6 tbsp olive oil

225 g/8 oz chorizo sausage, cut into 5-mm/¼-inch thick slices, casings removed

2 large onions, chopped

6 large garlic cloves, crushed

900 g/2 lb boned leg of lamb, cut into 5-cm/2-inch chunks

250 ml/9 fl oz lamb stock or water

125 ml/4 fl oz red wine, such as Rioja or Tempranillo

2 tbsp sherry vinegar

800 g/1 lb 12 oz canned chopped tomatoes

4 sprigs fresh thyme, plus extra to garnish

2 bay leaves

½ tsp sweet Spanish paprika

800 g/1 lb 12 oz canned chickpeas, rinsed and drained

salt and pepper

Preheat the oven to 160°C/325°F/Gas Mark 4. Heat 4 tablespoons of the oil in a large, heavy-based flameproof casserole over a medium–high heat. Reduce the heat, add the chorizo and fry for 1 minute. Transfer to a plate. Add the onions to the casserole and fry for 2 minutes, then add the garlic and continue frying for 3 minutes, or until the onions are soft, but not brown. Remove from the casserole and set aside.

Heat the remaining 2 tablespoons of oil in the casserole. Add the lamb cubes in a single layer without over-crowding the casserole, and fry until browned on each side; work in batches, if necessary.

Return the onion mixture and chorizo to the casserole with all the lamb. Stir in the stock, wine, vinegar, tomatoes with their juices and salt and pepper to taste. Bring to the boil, scraping any glazed bits from the base of the casserole. Reduce the heat and stir in the thyme, bay leaves and paprika.

Transfer to the preheated oven and cook, covered, for 40–45 minutes until the lamb is tender. Stir in the chickpeas and return to the oven, uncovered, for 10 minutes, or until they are heated through and the juices are reduced.

Taste and adjust the seasoning. Serve garnished with thyme.

Lamb Shanks

serves 6

1 tsp coriander seeds

1 tsp cumin seeds

1 tsp ground cinnamon

1 fresh green chilli, deseeded and finely chopped

1 garlic bulb, separated into cloves

125 ml/4 fl oz groundnut or sunflower oil

grated rind of 1 lime

6 lamb shanks

2 onions, chopped

2 carrots, chopped

2 celery sticks, chopped

1 lime, chopped

about 700 ml/1¼ pints beef stock or water

1 tsp sun-dried tomato purée

2 fresh mint sprigs

2 fresh rosemary sprigs, plus extra to garnish

salt and pepper

Dry-fry the coriander and cumin seeds until fragrant, then pound with the cinnamon, chilli and 2 garlic cloves in a mortar and pestle. Stir in half the oil and the lime rind. Rub the spice paste all over the lamb and marinate for 4 hours.

Preheat the oven to 200°C/400°F/Gas Mark 6. Heat the remaining oil in a flameproof casserole and cook the lamb, turning frequently, until evenly browned. Chop the remaining garlic and add to the casserole with the onions, carrots, celery and lime, then pour in enough stock or water to cover. Stir in the tomato purée, add the herbs and season with salt and pepper.

Cover and cook in the preheated oven for 30 minutes. Reduce the oven temperature to 160°C/325°F/Gas Mark 3 and cook for a further 3 hours, or until very tender.

Transfer the lamb to a dish. Strain the cooking liquid to remove any solids, then return the liquid to the casserole. Boil until reduced and thickened. Serve the lamb with the sauce poured over it, garnished with sprigs of rosemary.

Lamb with Mint

serves 4

2 tbsp sunflower oil

1 onion, chopped

1 garlic clove, finely chopped

1 tsp grated fresh ginger

1 tsp ground coriander

½ tsp chilli powder

¼ tsp ground turmeric

pinch of salt

350 g/12 oz fresh lamb mince

200 g/7 oz canned chopped tomatoes

1 tbsp chopped fresh mint

85 g/3 oz fresh or frozen peas

2 carrots, sliced into thin batons

1 fresh green chilli, deseeded and finely chopped

1 tbsp chopped fresh coriander

fresh mint sprigs, to garnish

Heat the oil in a large, heavy-based frying pan or flameproof casserole. Add the onion and cook over a low heat, stirring occasionally, for 10 minutes, or until golden.

Meanwhile, place the garlic, ginger, ground coriander, chilli powder, turmeric and salt in a small bowl and mix well. Add the spice mixture to the frying pan and cook, stirring constantly, for 2 minutes. Add the lamb and cook, stirring frequently, for 8–10 minutes, or until it is broken up and browned.

Add the tomatoes and their juices, the mint, peas, carrots, chilli and fresh coriander. Cook, stirring constantly, for 3–5 minutes, then serve, garnished with fresh mint sprigs.

Osso Bucco

serves 4

1 tbsp virgin olive oil

4 tbsp butter

2 onions, chopped

1 leek, sliced

3 tbsp plain flour

4 thick slices of veal shin (osso bucco)

300 ml/½ pint white wine

300 ml/½ pint veal or chicken stock

salt and pepper

gremolata

2 tbsp chopped fresh parsley

1 garlic clove, finely chopped

grated rind of 1 lemon

Heat the oil and butter in a large, heavy-based frying pan. Add the onions and leek and cook over a low heat, stirring occasionally, for 5 minutes, until softened.

Spread out the flour on a plate and season with salt and pepper. Toss the pieces of veal in the flour to coat, shaking off any excess. Add the veal to the frying pan, increase the heat to high and cook until browned on both sides.

Gradually stir in the wine and stock and bring just to the boil, stirring constantly. Lower the heat, cover and simmer for 1¼ hours, or until the veal is very tender.

Meanwhile, make the gremolata by mixing the parsley, garlic and lemon rind in a small bowl.

Transfer the veal to a warmed serving dish with a slotted spoon. Bring the sauce to the boil and cook, stirring occasionally, until thickened and reduced. Pour the sauce over the veal, sprinkle with the gremolata and serve immediately.

Poultry

Chicken Noodle Soup

serves 4–6

2 skinless chicken breasts

2 litres/3½ pints water

1 onion, unpeeled, halved

1 large garlic clove, halved

1-cm/½-inch piece fresh ginger, peeled and sliced

4 black peppercorns, lightly crushed

4 cloves

2 star anise

1 carrot, peeled

1 celery stick, chopped

100 g/3½ oz baby sweetcorn, halved lengthways

2 spring onions, finely shredded

115 g/4 oz dried rice vermicelli noodles

salt and pepper

Put the chicken breasts and water in a saucepan over a high heat and bring to the boil. Lower the heat to its lowest setting and simmer, skimming the surface until no more foam rises. Add the onion, garlic, ginger, peppercorns, cloves, star anise and a pinch of salt, and continue to simmer for 20 minutes, or until the chicken is tender and cooked through. Meanwhile, grate the carrot along its length on the coarse side of a grater so you get long, thin strips.

Strain the chicken, reserving about 1.2 litres/2 pints stock, but discarding any flavouring solids. (At this point you can leave the stock to cool and refrigerate overnight, so any fat solidifies and can be lifted off and discarded.) Return the stock to the rinsed-out saucepan with the carrot, celery, baby sweetcorn and spring onions and bring to the boil. Boil until the baby sweetcorn are almost tender, then add the noodles and continue boiling for 2 minutes.

Meanwhile, chop the chicken, add to the pan and continue cooking for about 1 minute longer until the chicken is reheated and the noodles are soft. Add seasoning to taste and serve.

Coq Au Vin

serves 4

55 g/2 oz butter

2 tbsp olive oil

1.8 kg/4 lb chicken pieces

115 g/4 oz rindless smoked bacon, cut into strips

115 g/4 oz baby onions

115 g/4 oz chestnut mushrooms, halved

2 garlic cloves, finely chopped

2 tbsp brandy

225 ml/8 fl oz red wine

300 ml/10 fl oz chicken stock

1 bouquet garni

2 tbsp plain flour

salt and pepper

bay leaves, to garnish

Melt half the butter with the olive oil in a large, flameproof casserole. Add the chicken and cook over a medium heat, stirring, for 8–10 minutes, or until golden brown all over. Add the bacon, onions, mushrooms and garlic.

Pour in the brandy and set it alight with a match or taper. When the flames have died down, add the wine, stock and bouquet garni and season to taste with salt and pepper. Bring to the boil, reduce the heat and simmer gently for 1 hour, or until the chicken pieces are cooked through and tender. Meanwhile, make a beurre manié by mashing the remaining butter with the flour in a small bowl.

Remove and discard the bouquet garni. Transfer the chicken to a large plate and keep warm. Stir the beurre manié into the casserole, a little at a time. Bring to the boil, return the chicken to the casserole and serve immediately, garnished with bay leaves.

Jambalaya

serves 4

2 tbsp vegetable oil

2 onions, roughly chopped

1 green pepper, deseeded and roughly chopped

2 celery sticks, roughly chopped

3 garlic cloves, finely chopped

2 tsp paprika

300 g/1½ oz skinless, boneless chicken breasts, chopped

100 g/3½ oz kabanos sausages, chopped

3 tomatoes, peeled and chopped

450 g/1 lb long-grain rice

850 ml/1½ pints hot chicken or fish stock

1 tsp dried oregano

2 bay leaves

12 large raw prawns

4 spring onions, finely chopped

2 tbsp chopped fresh parsley

salt and pepper

chopped fresh herbs, to garnish

Heat the vegetable oil in a large frying pan over a low heat. Add the onions, pepper, celery and garlic and cook for 8–10 minutes until all the vegetables have softened. Add the paprika and cook for a further 30 seconds. Add the chicken and sausages and cook for 8–10 minutes until lightly browned. Add the tomatoes and cook for 2–3 minutes until they have collapsed.

Add the rice to the pan and stir well. Pour in the hot stock, oregano and bay leaves and stir well. Cover and simmer for 10 minutes.

Add the prawns and stir. Cover again and cook for a further 6–8 minutes until the rice is tender and the prawns are cooked through.

Stir in the spring onions and parsley and season to taste with salt and pepper. Transfer to a large serving dish, garnish with chopped fresh herbs and serve.

Thai Green Chicken Curry

serves 4

2 tbsp groundnut or sunflower oil

2 tbsp ready-made Thai green curry paste

500 g/1 lb 2 oz skinless boneless chicken breasts, cut into cubes

2 kaffir lime leaves, roughly torn

1 lemon grass stalk, finely chopped

225 ml/8 fl oz canned coconut milk

16 baby aubergines, halved

2 tbsp Thai fish sauce

fresh Thai basil sprigs and kaffir lime leaves, thinly sliced, to garnish

Heat 2 tablespoons of oil in a preheated wok or large, heavy-based frying pan. Add 2 tablespoons of the curry paste and stir-fry briefly until all the aromas are released.

Add the chicken, lime leaves and lemon grass and stir-fry for 3–4 minutes, until the meat is beginning to colour. Add the coconut milk and aubergines and simmer gently for 8–10 minutes, or until tender.

Stir in the fish sauce and serve immediately, garnished with Thai basil sprigs and lime leaves.

Chicken Pasanda

serves 4

4 cardamom pods

6 black peppercorns

½ cinnamon stick

½ tsp cumin seeds

2 tsp garam masala

1 tsp chilli powder

1 tsp grated fresh ginger

1 garlic clove, very finely chopped

4 tbsp thick natural yogurt

pinch of salt

675 g/1 lb 8 oz skinless, boneless chicken, diced

5 tbsp groundnut oil

2 onions, finely chopped

3 fresh green chillies, deseeded and chopped

2 tbsp chopped fresh coriander

125 ml/4 fl oz single cream

fresh coriander sprigs, to garnish

Place the cardamom pods in a non-metallic dish with the peppercorns, cinnamon, cumin, garam masala, chilli powder, ginger, garlic, yogurt and salt. Add the chicken pieces and stir well to coat. Cover and leave to marinate in the refrigerator for 2–3 hours.

Heat the oil in a preheated wok or karahi. Add the onions and cook over a low heat, stirring occasionally, for 5 minutes, or until softened, then add the chicken pieces and marinade and cook over a medium heat, stirring, for 15 minutes, or until the chicken is cooked through.

Stir in the fresh chillies and coriander and pour in the cream. Heat through gently, but do not let it boil. Garnish with fresh coriander and serve immediately.

Chicken Tagine

serves 4

1 tbsp olive oil

1 onion, cut into small wedges

2–4 garlic cloves, sliced

450 g/1 lb skinless, boneless chicken breast, diced

1 tsp ground cumin

2 cinnamon sticks, lightly bruised

1 tbsp plain wholemeal flour

225 g/8 oz aubergine, diced

1 red pepper, deseeded and chopped

85 g/3 oz button mushrooms, sliced

1 tbsp tomato purée

600 ml/1 pint chicken stock

280 g/10 oz canned chickpeas, drained and rinsed

55 g/2 oz ready-to-eat dried apricots, chopped

salt and pepper

1 tbsp chopped fresh coriander, to garnish

Heat the oil in a large saucepan over a medium heat, add the onion and garlic and cook for 3 minutes, stirring frequently. Add the chicken and cook, stirring constantly, for a further 5 minutes, or until sealed on all sides. Add the cumin and cinnamon sticks to the saucepan halfway through sealing the chicken.

Sprinkle in the flour and cook, stirring constantly, for 2 minutes. Add the aubergine, red pepper and mushrooms and cook for a further 2 minutes, stirring constantly.

Blend the tomato purée with the stock, stir into the saucepan and bring to the boil. Reduce the heat and add the chickpeas and apricots. Cover and simmer for 15–20 minutes, or until the chicken is tender.

Season with salt and pepper to taste and serve immediately, sprinkled with coriander.

Italian-style Roast Chicken

serves 6

2.5 kg/5 lb 8 oz chicken

fresh rosemary sprigs

175 g/6 oz feta cheese, coarsely grated

2 tbsp sun-dried tomato purée

60 g/2 oz butter, softened

1 bulb garlic

1 kg/2 lb 4 oz new potatoes, halved if large

1 each red, green and yellow pepper, deseeded and cut into chunks

3 courgettes, thinly sliced

2 tbsp olive oil

2 tbsp plain flour

600 ml/1 pint chicken stock

salt and pepper

Preheat the oven to 190°C/375°F/Gas Mark 5. Rinse the chicken inside and out with cold water and drain well. Carefully cut between the skin and the top of the breast meat using a small pointed knife. Slide a finger into the slit and carefully enlarge it to form a pocket. Continue until the skin is completely lifted away from both breasts and the tops of the legs.

Chop the leaves from 3 rosemary stems. Mix with the feta cheese, sun-dried tomato purée, butter, and pepper to taste, then spoon under the skin. Put the chicken in a large roasting tin, cover with foil and cook in the preheated oven, calculating the cooking time as 20 minutes per 500 g/1 lb 2 oz, plus 20 minutes.

Break the garlic bulb into cloves but do not peel. Add the vegetables and garlic to the roasting tin. After 40 minutes, drizzle with oil, tuck in a few stems of rosemary and season with salt and pepper. Cook for the remaining calculated time, removing the foil for the last 40 minutes to brown the chicken.

Transfer the chicken to a serving platter. Place some of the vegetables around the chicken and transfer the remainder to a warmed serving dish. Spoon the fat out of the roasting tin (it will be floating on top) and stir the flour into the remaining cooking juices. Place the roasting tin on top of the hob and cook over a medium heat for 2 minutes, then gradually stir in the stock. Bring to the boil, stirring until thickened and season to taste. Strain into a gravy boat and serve with the chicken.

Spiced Chicken Stew

serves 6

1.8 kg/4 lb chicken pieces

2 tbsp paprika

2 tbsp olive oil

25 g/1 oz butter

450 g/1 lb onions, chopped

2 yellow peppers, deseeded and chopped

400 g/14 oz canned chopped tomatoes

225 ml/8 fl oz dry white wine

450 ml/16 fl oz chicken stock

1 tbsp Worcestershire sauce

½ tsp Tabasco Sauce

1 tbsp finely chopped fresh parsley

325 g/11½ oz canned sweetcorn kernels, drained

425 g/15 oz canned butter beans, drained and rinsed

2 tbsp plain flour

4 tbsp water

salt

fresh parsley sprigs, to garnish

Season the chicken pieces with salt and dust with paprika. Heat the oil and butter in a flameproof casserole or large saucepan. Add the chicken pieces and cook over a medium heat, turning, for 10–15 minutes, or until golden. Transfer to a plate with a slotted spoon.

Add the onion and peppers to the casserole. Cook over a low heat, stirring occasionally, for 5 minutes, or until softened.

Add the tomatoes, wine, stock, Worcestershire sauce, Tabasco sauce and parsley and bring to the boil, stirring. Return the chicken to the casserole, cover and simmer, stirring occasionally, for 30 minutes.

Add the sweetcorn and beans to the casserole, partially re-cover and simmer for a further 30 minutes. Place the flour and water in a small bowl and mix to make a paste. Stir a ladleful of the cooking liquid into the paste, then stir the paste into the stew. Cook, stirring frequently, for 5 minutes. Serve, garnished with parsley.

Chicken & Barley Stew

serves 4

2 tbsp vegetable oil

8 small, skinless chicken thighs

500 ml/18 fl oz chicken stock

100 g/3½ oz pearl barley, rinsed and drained

200 g/7 oz small new potatoes, scrubbed and halved lengthways

2 large carrots, peeled and sliced

1 leek, trimmed and sliced

2 shallots, sliced

1 tbsp tomato purée

1 bay leaf

1 courgette, trimmed and sliced

2 tbsp chopped fresh flat-leaf parsley, plus extra sprigs to garnish

2 tbsp plain flour

4 tbsp water

salt and pepper

Heat the oil in a large saucepan over a medium heat. Add the chicken and cook for 3 minutes, then turn over and cook on the other side for a further 2 minutes. Add the stock, barley, potatoes, carrots, leek, shallots, tomato purée and bay leaf. Bring to the boil, lower the heat and simmer for 30 minutes.

Add the courgette and chopped parsley, cover the pan and cook for a further 20 minutes, or until the chicken is cooked through. Remove the bay leaf and discard.

In a separate bowl, mix the flour with 4 tablespoons of water and stir into a smooth paste. Add it to the stew and cook, stirring, over a low heat for a further 5 minutes. Season to taste with salt and pepper.

Remove from the heat, ladle into individual serving bowls and garnish with sprigs of fresh parsley.

Florida Chicken

serves 4

450 g/1 lb skinless, boneless chicken

1½ tbsp plain flour

1 tbsp olive oil

1 onion, cut into wedges

2 celery sticks, sliced

150 ml/5 fl oz orange juice

300 ml/10 fl oz chicken stock

1 tbsp light soy sauce

1–2 tsp clear honey

1 tbsp grated orange rind

1 orange pepper, deseeded and chopped

225 g/8 oz courgettes, sliced into half moons

2 small corn on the cob, halved, or 100 g/3½ oz baby sweetcorn

1 orange, peeled and segmented

salt and pepper

1 tbsp chopped fresh parsley, to garnish

Lightly rinse the chicken and pat dry with kitchen paper. Cut into bite-sized pieces. Season the flour well with salt and pepper. Toss the chicken in the seasoned flour until well coated and reserve any remaining seasoned flour.

Heat the oil in a large, heavy-based frying pan and cook the chicken over a high heat, stirring frequently, for 5 minutes, or until golden on all sides and sealed. Using a slotted spoon, transfer the chicken to a plate.

Add the onion and celery to the frying pan and cook over a medium heat, stirring frequently, for 5 minutes, or until softened. Sprinkle in the reserved seasoned flour and cook, stirring constantly, for 2 minutes, then remove from the heat. Gradually stir in the orange juice, stock, soy sauce and honey, followed by the orange rind, then return to the heat and bring to the boil, stirring.

Return the chicken to the frying pan. Reduce the heat, cover and simmer, stirring occasionally, for 15 minutes. Add the orange pepper, courgettes and corn on the cob and simmer for a further 10 minutes, or until the chicken and vegetables are tender. Add the orange segments, stir well and heat through for 1 minute. Serve garnished with the parsley.

Red Hot Chilli Chicken

serves 4

1 tbsp curry paste

2 fresh green chillies, chopped

5 dried red chillies

2 tbsp tomato purée

2 garlic cloves, chopped

1 tsp chilli powder

pinch of sugar

pinch of salt

2 tbsp groundnut or sunflower oil

½ tsp cumin seeds

1 onion, chopped

2 curry leaves

1 tsp ground cumin

1 tsp ground coriander

½ tsp ground turmeric

400 g/14 oz canned chopped tomatoes

150 ml/5 fl oz chicken stock

4 skinless, boneless chicken breasts

1 tsp garam masala

freshly cooked rice

fresh mint sprigs, to garnish

To make the chilli paste, place the curry paste, fresh and dried chillies, tomato purée, garlic, chilli powder and sugar in a blender or food processor and add a pinch of salt. Process into a smooth paste.

Heat the oil in a large, heavy-based saucepan. Add the cumin seeds and cook over a medium heat, stirring constantly, for 2 minutes, or until they begin to pop and release their aroma. Add the onion and curry leaves and cook, stirring, for 5 minutes.

Add the chilli paste and cook for 2 minutes, then stir in the ground cumin, coriander and turmeric and cook for a further 2 minutes.

Add the tomatoes and their juices and the stock. Bring to the boil, then reduce the heat and simmer for 5 minutes. Add the chicken and garam masala, cover and simmer gently for 20 minutes, or until the chicken is cooked through and tender. Serve immediately with rice and garnished with fresh mint sprigs.

Pappardelle with Chicken & Porcini

serves 4

40 g/1½ oz dried porcini mushrooms

175 ml/6 fl oz hot water

800 g/1 lb 12 oz canned chopped tomatoes

1 fresh red chilli, deseeded and finely chopped

3 tbsp olive oil

350 g/12 oz skinless, boneless chicken, cut into thin strips

2 garlic cloves, finely chopped

350 g/12 oz dried pappardelle

salt and pepper

2 tbsp chopped fresh flat-leaf parsley, to garnish

Place the porcini in a small bowl, add the hot water and leave to soak for 20 minutes. Meanwhile, place the tomatoes and their can juices in a heavy-based saucepan and break them up with a wooden spoon, then stir in the chilli. Bring to the boil, reduce the heat and simmer, stirring occasionally, for 30 minutes, or until reduced.

Remove the mushrooms from their soaking liquid with a perforated spoon, reserving the liquid. Sieve the liquid through a coffee filter paper or muslin-lined sieve into the tomatoes and simmer for a further 15 minutes.

Meanwhile, heat 2 tablespoons of the olive oil in a heavy-based frying pan. Add the chicken and cook, stirring frequently, until golden brown all over and tender. Stir in the mushrooms and garlic and cook for a further 5 minutes.

While the chicken is cooking, bring a large, heavy-based saucepan of lightly salted water to the boil. Add the pasta, return to the boil and cook for 8–10 minutes, or until tender but still firm to the bite. Drain well, transfer to a warmed serving dish, drizzle with the remaining olive oil and toss lightly. Stir the chicken mixture into the tomato sauce, season to taste with salt and pepper and spoon on top of the pasta. Toss lightly, sprinkle with parsley and serve immediately.

Turkey & Lentil Soup

serves 4

1 tbsp olive oil

1 garlic clove, chopped

1 large onion, chopped

200 g/7 oz mushrooms, sliced

1 red pepper, deseeded and chopped

6 tomatoes, peeled, deseeded and chopped

1.2 litres/2 pints chicken stock

150 ml/5 fl oz red wine

85 g/3 oz cauliflower florets

1 carrot, chopped

200 g/7 oz red lentils

350 g/12 oz cooked turkey, chopped

1 courgette, chopped

1 tbsp shredded fresh basil

salt and pepper

sprigs of fresh basil, to garnish

Heat the oil in a large saucepan. Add the garlic and onion and cook over a medium heat, stirring, for 3 minutes, until slightly softened. Add the mushrooms, red pepper and tomatoes and cook for a further 5 minutes, stirring. Pour in the stock and red wine, then add the cauliflower, carrot and red lentils. Season to taste with salt and pepper. Bring to the boil, then lower the heat and simmer the soup gently for 25 minutes, until the vegetables are tender and cooked through.

Add the turkey and courgette to the pan and cook for 10 minutes. Stir in the shredded basil and cook for a further 5 minutes, then remove from the heat and ladle into serving bowls. Garnish with basil and serve immediately.

Mexican Turkey

serves 4

55 g/2 oz plain flour

4 turkey breast fillets

3 tbsp corn oil

1 onion, thinly sliced

1 red pepper, deseeded and sliced

300 ml/10 fl oz chicken stock

25 g/1 oz raisins

4 tomatoes, peeled, deseeded and chopped

1 tsp chilli powder

½ tsp ground cinnamon

pinch of ground cumin

25 g/1 oz plain chocolate, finely chopped or grated

salt and pepper

sprigs of fresh coriander, to garnish

Preheat the oven to 160°C/325°F/Gas Mark 3. Spread the flour on a plate and season with salt and pepper. Coat the turkey fillets in the seasoned flour, shaking off any excess. Reserve any remaining seasoned flour.

Heat the oil in a flameproof casserole. Add the turkey fillets and cook over a medium heat, turning occasionally, for 5–10 minutes, or until golden. Transfer to a plate with a slotted spoon.

Add the onion and red pepper to the casserole. Cook over a low heat, stirring occasionally, for 5 minutes, or until softened. Sprinkle in the remaining seasoned flour and cook, stirring constantly, for 1 minute. Gradually stir in the stock, then add the raisins, chopped tomatoes, chilli powder, cinnamon, cumin and chocolate. Season to taste with salt and pepper. Bring to the boil, stirring constantly.

Return the turkey to the casserole, cover and cook in the preheated oven for 50 minutes. Serve immediately, garnished with sprigs of coriander.

Italian Turkey Cutlets

serves 4

1 tbsp olive oil

4 turkey escalopes or steaks

2 red peppers, deseeded and sliced

1 red onion, sliced

2 garlic cloves, finely chopped

300 ml/10 fl oz passata

150 ml/5 fl oz medium white wine

1 tbsp chopped fresh marjoram

400 g/14 oz canned cannellini beans, drained and rinsed

3 tbsp fresh white breadcrumbs

salt and pepper

fresh basil sprigs, to garnish

Preheat the grill to medium. Heat the oil in a flameproof casserole or heavy-based frying pan. Add the turkey escalopes and cook over a medium heat for 5–10 minutes, turning occasionally, until golden. Transfer to a plate.

Add the red pepper and onion to the frying pan and cook over a low heat, stirring occasionally, for 5 minutes, or until softened. Add the garlic and cook for a further 2 minutes.

Return the turkey to the frying pan and add the passata, wine and marjoram. Season to taste with salt and pepper. Bring to the boil, then reduce the heat, cover and simmer, stirring occasionally, for 25–30 minutes, or until the turkey is cooked through and tender.

Stir in the cannellini beans and simmer for a further 5 minutes. Sprinkle the breadcrumbs over the top and place under the preheated grill for 2–3 minutes, or until golden. Serve, garnished with fresh basil sprigs.

Duck with Spring Onion Soup

serves 2

2 duck breasts, skin on

2 tbsp red curry paste

2 tbsp vegetable or
groundnut oil

bunch of spring onions,
chopped

2 garlic cloves, crushed

5-cm/2-inch piece fresh
ginger, grated

2 carrots, thinly sliced

1 red pepper, deseeded and
cut into strips

1 litre/1¼ pints chicken
stock

2 tbsp sweet chilli sauce

3–4 tbsp Thai soy sauce

400 g/14 oz canned straw
mushrooms, drained

Slash the skin of the duck 3 or 4 times with a sharp knife and rub in the curry paste. Cook the duck breasts, skin-side down, in a wok or frying pan over a high heat for 2–3 minutes. Turn over, reduce the heat and cook for a further 3–4 minutes, until cooked through. Lift out and slice thickly. Set aside and keep warm.

Meanwhile, heat the oil in a wok or large frying pan and stir-fry half the spring onions, the garlic, ginger, carrots and red pepper for 2–3 minutes. Pour in the stock and add the chilli sauce, soy sauce and mushrooms. Bring to the boil, lower the heat and simmer for 4–5 minutes.

Ladle the soup into warmed bowls, top with the duck slices and garnish with the remaining spring onions. Serve immediately.

Duck Legs with Olives

serves 4

4 duck legs, all visible fat trimmed off

800 g/1 lb 12 oz canned tomatoes, chopped

8 garlic cloves, peeled but left whole

1 large onion, chopped

1 carrot, finely chopped

1 celery stick, finely chopped

3 sprigs fresh thyme

100 g/3½ oz Spanish green olives in brine, stuffed with pimientos, garlic or almonds, drained and rinsed

1 tsp finely grated orange rind

salt and pepper

Put the duck legs in the bottom of a flameproof casserole or a large, heavy-based frying pan with a tight-fitting lid. Add the tomatoes, garlic, onion, carrot, celery, thyme and olives and stir together. Season to taste with salt and pepper.

Turn the heat to high and cook, uncovered, until the ingredients begin to bubble. Reduce the heat to low, cover tightly and simmer for 1¼–1½ hours until the duck is very tender. Check occasionally and add a little water if the mixture appears to be drying out.

When the duck is tender, transfer it to a serving platter, cover and keep hot in a preheated warm oven. Leave the casserole uncovered, increase the heat to medium and cook, stirring, for about 10 minutes until the mixture forms a sauce. Stir in the orange rind, then taste and adjust the seasoning if necessary.

Mash the tender garlic cloves with a fork and spread over the duck legs. Spoon the sauce over the top. Serve at once.

Duck Jambalaya-style Stew

serves 4

4 duck breasts, about 150 g/5½ oz each

2 tbsp olive oil

225 g/8 oz piece gammon, cut into small chunks

225 g/8 oz chorizo, outer casing removed

1 onion, chopped

3 garlic cloves, chopped

3 celery sticks, chopped

1–2 fresh red chillies, deseeded and chopped

1 green pepper, deseeded and chopped

600 ml/1 pint chicken stock

1 tbsp chopped fresh oregano

400 g/14 oz canned chopped tomatoes

1–2 tsp hot pepper sauce, or to taste

chopped fresh flat-leaf parsley, to garnish

green salad and freshly cooked rice, to serve

Remove and discard the skin and any fat from the duck breasts. Cut the flesh into bite-sized pieces.

Heat half the oil in a large deep frying pan and cook the duck, gammon and chorizo over a high heat, stirring frequently, for 5 minutes, or until browned on all sides and sealed. Using a slotted spoon, remove from the frying pan and set aside.

Add the onion, garlic, celery and chillies to the frying pan and cook over a medium heat, stirring frequently, for 5 minutes, or until softened. Add the green pepper, then stir in the stock, oregano, tomatoes and hot pepper sauce. Bring to the boil, then reduce the heat and return the duck, gammon and chorizo to the frying pan. Cover and simmer, stirring occasionally, for 20 minutes, or until the duck and gammon are tender.

Serve immediately, garnished with parsley and accompanied by a green salad and rice.